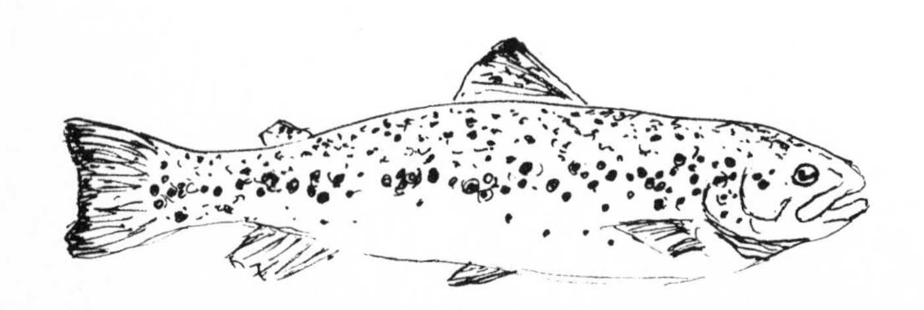

MARGARET ASHBY

The Hook to Cook Book

Recipes for Trout, Sea Trout and Salmon

H. F. & G. Witherby Ltd.

First Published 1985 by H. F. & G. Witherby Ltd,
32 Aylesbury Street, Clerkenwell Green, EC1R 0ET

ISBN 0 85493 145 7

Printed in Great Britain by BAS Printers Limited,
Over Wallop, Hampshire

This little book is dedicated to my husband who has provided me with such beautiful game fish over the years.

I hope it will encourage others to make the best of the fish they catch, and to explore cooking possibilities beyond the grillpan.

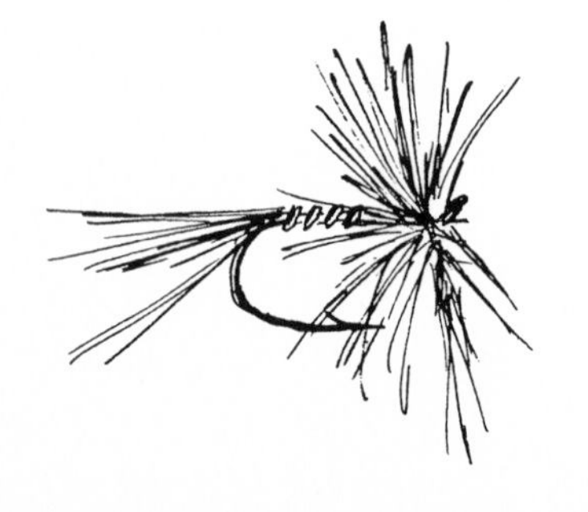

Introduction

The reason I decided to write this little game fish cookery book, was that whenever I asked the successful angler how he hoped to have his fish cooked, he would look a bit blank and say he would probably have it grilled as usual. If I suggested a recipe to him, he would smile and say that they hadn't thought of doing that to a trout.

But I'm sure most anglers are like my husband, who has the most beautiful rods, superb reels, and exquisite flies. Surely the fish, for which all this expensive gear is to be used, does deserve a better fate than just a grill pan. The better the fish the better the recipe.

The same goes for the supporting drink. What is a bottle of wine at the end of the day, when the rod costs the earth? As a female I think it is a question of priorities.

Taste is everything! These precious fish deserve the best ingredients. Use fresh crisp herbs, and the best vegetables you can find, cooked with great care, so as to preserve the flavour and as much goodness as possible, with the minimum of cooking, or not at all. These fish have such a delicate flavour, that it is so easy to spoil it, or at least overpower it instead of enhancing it.

Also I do like the fish to look as nice when cooked as when it was alive – only different. Colour is very important. Where else would you see that lovely pink fish, with the superb texture.

So do enjoy cooking it, just as much as the angler had pleasure in catching it. In fact, a double pleasure, shared.

Bon appétit!

Contents

Acknowledgements

Elisabeth Ayrton's wonderful book *The Cookery of England* changed my whole attitude to cooking, not ony by filling in the 'pedigree' of some of my traditional recipes, but by inspiring me to become more adventurous in cooking. It hands on to the reader the truly great cookery which is our heritage.

My thanks are due to Dorothy Dickens for providing the attractive drawings.

I am also deeply grateful to the very talented but kind and patient chefs, who although so busy, still managed to find time to take me, stage by stage, through their recipes, or had them so carefully typed out for me. I always thought chefs were very temperamental, but the men I met were marvellous. They are: Richard Ferebee of The Falcon, Uppingham; Nicholas Gill, of Hambleton Hall (Egon Ronay's Restaurant of the Year); Nicholas Healey of The Noel Arms, Whitwell; Victor Morgado, The Bull and Swan, Stamford; Manuel Pinto of the lovely cellar restaurant, The Candlesticks, Stamford; and especially Richard Brandrick and Graham Jones, of the Haycock, Wansford for the practical advice and help given.

Lastly I am indebted to Marcus Warwick, professional Rod Maker, for his recipes and useful tips on fish cookery.

1 Game Fish

Atlantic Salmon

Caught in the waters round the British Isles, it is highly thought of for its fine flavour and special quality.

Salmon are beautiful fish, and easy to identify. The body is rounded, and the head quite small. The tail is definitely forked. The skin steely grey on the back, silvery white on the belly, all of it gleaming. A smattering of black spots show above the lateral line. The weight can be anything from 7 lb to 20 lbs, sometimes much more.

Grilse

The name given to young salmon, returning early to its native river to spawn for the first time. It looks just what it is, a small salmon, usually under 7 lbs. Grilse can be cooked in any of the ways suitable for other game fish, although its size does make it ideal for small dinner parties.

Sea Trout or Salmon Trout

This fish is considered to have the finest flavour of all our game fish, having the best qualities of both the salmon and trout. The shape is beautifully streamlined, and the skin is very silvery, with spots all over. The tail is not forked and the head is less pointed than the salmon. The average weight is 2 lbs to 4 lbs, although they can reach 10 lbs or more.

Rainbow Trout
A fish introduced to other parts of the world including the British Isles, from North America. An elegant fish distinguished by a rosy band which runs down the side of the fish, and by the fact that its black spots are found on the tail as well as the body. Dark fish caught early in the season are not good for eating. A well conditioned fish is bright silver except for its typical rosy lateral sheen. Typical weight is 1 lb to 4 lbs, and fish between these weights are best for eating. Rainbow may however, weigh much more, and still be excellent for cooking.

Brown Trout
This is the trout native to our fresh waters in the British Isles. Its usual colouring is browner than the rainbow. Its sides are heavily spotted with red or black spots: the spots do not, however, extend to include the tail. Typical weight is half a pound to 2 lbs in rivers and perhaps 1 lb to 5 lbs in reservoirs. Once again these fish may grow to a far greater weight, but the biggest fish are not always the best for eating.

Grayling
A fish which is fairly local in its distribution. Easily recognisable by its uniform grey-green and silver colour and its large sail-like dorsal fin. It is usually spotted a little on the sides. Weight is from 1 lb to 3 lbs. It is highly prized as a table fish.

From the angler's and cook's point of view one of its chief attractions is that it is at its best when the trout is out of season, in the autumn and winter months.

Other Salmonidae
Also included among fish of the trout and salmon type are American Brook Trout, Char and various white fishes (Vendace, Powan, etc.).

The American brook trout is becoming more common. It is excellent to eat and any recipe suitable for small brown trout will do. The char and white fishes have become too scarce to warrant separate recipes in this small book, except for a reference to potted char.

Farmed Fish
Most fish of the salmon family (salmon or trout) can today be readily bred in fish farms. Most rainbow and brown trout available in fish shops will be these farm fish. Many salmon on the slab in the shop will also have been artificially bred and reared. In the case of salmon, wild fish and farmed fish should be identified as such by the fishmonger and the price of the wild fish will be higher than that of farmed fish.

Farmed fish should be reasonably good to eat, but the flavour will never equal that of wild fish.

Farmed fish of all types can usually be recognised by their mis-shapen and under-developed fins, especially tail fins.

2 General Notes on Cooking Fish

The Fisherman's Part in the Cooking Business

The experienced angler should skip this and hand the recipes to his wife. These few notes are for angling beginners and those who are not too sure about caring for fish in the pre-kitchen phase.

Game fish intended for the table, when netted or beached should be killed as soon as possible, by one or two sharp blows on the skull. This is best done before removing the hook and the blows do need to be on the skull, not on the flesh behind the skull. Blows on the flesh are both ineffective and damage the flesh for culinary purposes.

Fish when killed should at once be transferred to a bass. These are sold in all good tackle shops. The bass should be well soused with water, and placed in the shade. Things to avoid are placing the fish in rubber or plastic bags, leaving them at the waterside under water or worse still, leaving them about on the bank, particularly in the sun. The general principle is to keep them away from heat, sunlight, flies, animal predators, and two legged thieves. The fish bass is best of all, and it should be immersed in water at regular intervals so that it is moist throughout the day. The evaporation of the water helps to cool the fish.

As soon as the fish are got home, they should

be scaled, cleaned and gutted. Scaling of game fish is not essential. We always eat the skin, and find it quite as good unscaled as scaled. However, we are sure, for the sake of others, scales are best removed, and certainly if trout from your water have a muddy flavour; the scales do hold that taste. The cleanest way of scaling is to fill a fair-sized sink with water and scrape the fish with a knife from tail to head under water. This prevents the scales flying all over the kitchen. If a fish has dried out, let it soak for a few minutes before scaling.

Head and fins can be left on fish during cooking. A fish presents more of a spectacle when served 'entire', and a specimen fish for a special occasion should have head and tail left on. In general, however, remove fins, tail and head. In any case a large fish without head and tail is certainly easier to fit into a pan or kettle. Tails and fins can usually be removed with large sharp kitchen scissors or poultry shears. The head should be removed with a sharp knife, the fish being laid on a board if necessary.

The fish is now to be gutted. The fish is slit up the belly from vent to head, and the guts pulled out from the belly starting at the vent end. To remove the guts from the body, the oesophagus needs to be snipped with the kitchen scissors at the head end. This to an angler is the interesting part of the business, for at this stage one can immediately squeeze the contents of the stomach out through the severed oesphagus into a white cup. A little water is added and as the food mass floats apart one can see in detail the food intake of the fish.

Finally remove the dark blood-like organ lying inside the body cavity, down the backbone. This is easily removed with the thumbnail, holding the fish under running water.

The fish which has now been scaled, cleaned, gutted and beheaded should lastly be lightly dried with a kitchen cloth or paper towelling. It is now ready for cooking or freezing.

A few final words for the novice. When you start to clean fish, have plenty of old newspapers ready to receive the guts and fins. Use a very sharp flexible bladed knife. In all these operations a razor sharp blade is essential. As regards filleting the main principle is to start with a straight deep cut down the centre line of the back, from head to tail. This acts as a guide to the knife for the rest of the operation. Work from head to tail, running the knife along to separate flesh from backbone, one side at a time. While filleting the fish can be steadied on the board by holding the head with the free hand, or by placing the free hand flat on the flank of the fish immediately above the point where the blade is working. It needs practice before a good clean job can be achieved by any of the various methods in use. Mind your fingers!

Notes on Cooking

However good your fishmonger, he will never produce anything up to the standard of your own catch. Preferably eat your fish as soon as possible, but if they are to be frozen, clean and freeze without delay. All the best fishing hotels provide freezing facilities, as do some large reservoirs.

There is no substitute for butter in the cooking of game fish, and even in these cholesterol conscious days, it is still the only thing to use. Nothing else is quite right in either flavour or texture.

We also find with wine that a good dry wine is definitely better than the so called cooking wine. In fact we use the wine we are going to drink with the meal.

Herbs are very important in fish cookery and there again, the fresh ones collected out of the garden just as they are needed, have no substitute. They are so easy to grow, even in a small courtyard.

When serving cold smoked salmon or trout at a party, serve from a bed of freshly picked herbs. Fennel or dill are good, they will keep the bread moist and add a decorative touch. Don't forget to garnish with parsley, which is a 'must' for any fish dish, the crisper and greener the better.

A well known firm now produces fish stock cubes, which I find excellent.

Trout caught in waters that have a muddy taste can be improved by soaking in salt water with a good dash of wine vinegar. Leave for 2–3 hours and then dry and treat as normal trout. Perhaps it is a good idea to be a little more generous however with the lemon juice or wine when cooking such fish. These fish do need to be scaled, as the scales can hold the muddy flavour.

Never spoil game fish cookery with malt vinegar. Wine vinegar is better. Dry cider can be quite a good alternative.

Sea salt is better than Cooking salt. Fresh ground pepper is a 'must'. Nutmeg and mace are the best spices.

As for frozen game fish, it is better to defrost in the refrigerator, leaving the fish wrapped in its packing. A rough guide is 18 hours for a fish weighing up to 4 lbs, and 24 to 36 hours for a medium sized whole fish. If you are pushed for time leave the fish at room temperature allowing 4 hours per pound.

Although I prefer to thaw mine, steaks and

cutlets can be cooked from frozen, but allow a longer cooking time.

A final word about presentation of cooked fish to the table. Some cooks have recommended that the skin should be removed. Do leave the skin on. It helps to keep the flesh moist, and connoisseurs usually think it a necessary part of the dish.

Handling and Serving Cooked Game Fish

Handling cooked fish is every bit as tricky as coping with them when first caught.

Some wrap their fish in muslin or greaseproof paper when poaching. Apart from keeping body and soul together if you have cooked them, I can't think this serves any useful purpose. To me it is an added hazard.

For fish to be served cold, leave in the kettle or baking dish until almost cold, then lift out with well scrubbed hands and if it is a big beast, preferably have a spare pair of hands standing by. If using a traditional kettle, instead of using hands, lift out on trivet and place crosswise over kettle. Scrape the skin and subcutaneous tissue off, (leaving head and tail intact) using the back of a knife working from head to tail. It is normally necessary to skin only the upper side.

For fish to be dressed for a buffet, the backbone can be removed, but I would place the fish on the serving plate first, because it will have less stability after the operation. Ease the flesh just below the head and very carefully snip the backbone with kitchen scissors. Do the same just above the tail. Cut the flesh through to the bone from head to tail, and it should be possible to gently pull the backbone out intact.

When a poached fish is to be served hot, hands alone cannot be used to lift out the fish so if you are not using a kettle with trivet you have to use two suitable kitchen 'slices' to remove it from the liquid. If it is a big fish you need someone standing by as close as possible with the dish.

When fish baked in the oven are to be placed on a serving dish it is very important that you grease or oil the baking dish well before cooking to prevent 'sticking'. It is in fact often worth cooking the fish in the dish from which it is to be served. The juices can be poured off to make a sauce more easily than the fish can be lifted. The importance of greasing the baking dish also applies to foil cooked fish.

Regarding foil baking, I find it best to place the fish still in foil on the serving dish. The foil can then be cut with a pair of scissors and carefully slid away to leave the fish intact. If the liquids in the foil are to be used for making a sauce, one end of the parcel is opened to allow the juices to drain out into a container before the parcel is placed on the dish.

Now comes the question of actually serving the fish onto the plate. In general, except in the case of boned fish already mentioned, the method is to serve the upper half first, using the back bone as a base against which to cut each portion. When the whole of the upper half has been taken, the head, backbone and tail are carefully lifted off, using a knife as necessary to ease the flesh of the lower half from the bone.

For serving you cannot beat a set of fish servers. Nice old ones can be picked up quite cheaply. We bought ours at auction, complete with silver mounted horn handles, for a pound.

A final word. Check carefully portions intended for the very young and the very old to see that bones are removed. Neither age group can cope with bones, which can put children off fish for life!

Smoking Fish

There are many smokers available on the market. Instructions supplied with these smokers are not always adequate. Here are a few tips.

Small home smokers, which are literally small metal boxes, usually use the 'hot smoking' procedure. With these smokers the easiest procedure is to fillet trout before smoking if of 1½ lb weight or over. Smaller trout may be smoked whole. Do not overload the smoker. Most small smokers will take 4 to 6 fillets.

The procedure is divided into three stages – salting, 'drying' or airing, and smoking. Each stage takes from 1 to 1½ hours.

To salt, place adequate salt on a large dish, lay the fillets on the salt and rub additional salt on the upper surface. A little dark brown sugar can be rubbed in with the salt if desired to add flavour. Leave for upwards of 1 hour.

Now comes the drying or airing process. Start by washing off excess salt under a tap and pat dry with kitchen paper. Now hang up the fish (using metal hooks if available) in the shade in moving air, if possible. Leave once again for at least 1 hour and wiping from time to time to remove moisture will aid the process.

Lastly the smoking proper. Smoke for at least one hour in plentiful smoke. It will not work if either the sawdust or methylated spirit burner runs out too soon. The supply of sawdust loaded for the operation must be adequate and the burner may have to be refilled half way through.

Some smokers involve the fish being laid on a grid. This is a simple operation, but if your smoker is one (like ours) where the fish are hung in the smoke box from metal bars placed across the top then unless care is taken, fish break up during the operation and fall from the bars into the sawdust. Suspended fish need to be placed in a sling of cooking twine, so that they are not suspended from a single point.

Excellent results can be obtained with a little care using a cheap simple proprietary smoker.

Generally speaking, where salmon are concerned, the professional smoke houses do a better job than the amateur.

If you have not been lucky with your salmon fishing and the shop-smoked salmon is mediocre, the Summer Isles Smoke Houses at Achiltibuei, do a very good mail order service, supplying first class salmon/trout/eel, etc., etc. They do an excellent service in the North-west Highlands, collecting fish caught that day, smoking and either delivering back or posting on. Their smoking technique is second to none.

The results produced by professional smoking vary from one place to another, so do shop around.

For those of us who live South of the Border, the smoke house at Orford, Suffolk, is another well known professional smoke house, whose products are excellent. They also will send their smoked fish by post to individual purchasers and will smoke any fish taken to them. The address is The Butley Orford Oysterage, Orford, Suffolk.

Another firm to be recommended is The Coln Valley Smokery, Winson, Cirencester, Glos., GL7 5ER, who have taken what they describe as 'a positive step backwards', and use traditional kilns. Their 'Cotswold Cure' uses nothing but salt, sugar and oakwood smoke. The results are distinctive and delicious.

Wines for Drinking with Fish Dishes

For smoked fish dishes, starters or main courses, pale dry sherry is ideal. Some of us (but not all) also enjoy Greek Retsina.

As no strong dressings are used with other fish dishes, all the light dry wines (well chilled) are suitable. Such wines are Vinho Verde (Portuguese), Verdicchio and Soave (Italian), Chablis (French), Gewürztraminer (Alsace), various Hocks (German) and white Rioja (Spanish). Rosé wines will go with fish dishes if you do not have a palate for dry wines.

For those who do not fancy wine in any shape or form, dry cider is good not only for cooking itself, but to drink with the fish dish. For beer, dry lager such as Diat Pils is our choice, but beer drinkers tend to have their own prejudices which brook no interference.

For smoked prime salmon, don't forget that the lovely peaty malts are a natural choice. Try Laphroaig, Taliska or the Macallan.

3 Roasting and Baking

Baked Stuffed Salmon or Sea Trout, with English Sauce
(Traditional)

The stuffing for this dish is more or less the same as we use in the pike my husband hooks from time to time.

4–5 lb Sea Trout, Salmon or Trout
$\frac{1}{4}$ lb fine bread crumbs, soaked in milk
2 anchovy fillets pounded, or essence
4 oz sautéd pink mushrooms
Fresh herbs of your choice finely chopped
Salt and pepper to taste
(Prawns can be substituted for anchovy fillets and sliced green olives are an interesting option)

Clean and dry fish, wipe cavity with lemon juice or tarragon vinegar. Squeeze excess milk out of soaked breadcrumbs and add the finely chopped herbs, sautéd mushrooms and the butter they were cooked in. Traditionally anchovies are added next, but especially for sea trout with their delicate flavour, we prefer prawns. It is just a question of preference. Season to taste, mix well and stuff the cavity with the mixture. If on the dry side add another knob of butter. Secure with cocktail sticks. Wrap in oiled foil and place on baking tray or dish. Cook in preheated oven 375°F for 45 minutes. Test with fork to ensure it is cooked as ovens vary so much.

Serve with English Sauce. (See Sauce Recipe, page 69).

Baked Salmon with Oyster Stuffing

Another lovely old recipe from about the middle of the last century. Personally I think the old recipes are so much better than modern day ones. I think the quality of ingredients must have been the most important thing. As this dish uses the tail end of the fish you can freeze the steaks.

Tail end of fish weighing 2–3 lbs and filleted
Oysters or a tin if fresh ones not available
1 heaped tablespoon finely chopped parsley
4 oz fine bread crumbs
4 oz butter
1 egg yolk beaten
2 glasses dry white wine
¼ pint double cream
good pinch nutmeg
mace ground (a good pinch)
Seasoning to taste

Put the oysters in a bowl complete with liquid. Add the parsley, breadcrumbs, seasoning and spices. Beat into this mix 3 oz of the butter and the egg yolk. Prepare the fillets and lay flat. Spread the mixture over one half. Do not go too near the edge. Place second fillet on top, and secure with kitchen string, to keep the filling in place. Put the fillets in baking dish, dot the remaining butter and seasoning on top. Cover with foil. Bake in a hot oven 400°F for about 45 minutes. When cooked place on warm serving dish. Add the cream to the liquor and stir in. Pour this over fillets. Serve at once, removing string first.

Small new potatoes and possibly barely cooked sliced green beans, would go well with this lovely dish.

Celebration Salmon, Sea Trout or Trout

This is a really luxurious recipe. You may just be rejoicing at having landed the best fish ever, in which case this dish is a must. It is an Edwardian idea for their large and lavish dinner parties preceding their even more glamorous balls. They used several fish, but I think even fish were more plentiful in those days.

1 salmon, sea trout, or trout about 3 lb is ideal
½ pint of double cream
2 glasses dry Champagne or a dry sparkling wine
Seasoned flour
1 cucumber cut into neat cubes
Butter for cooking

Clean and gut the fish, wipe dry. The Edwardians skinned theirs. Well butter an ovenproof dish, lay the prepared fish in and spoon or brush the thick cream over the fish. Sprinkle the seasoned flour over the cream. Place in preheated oven 375°F and cook for 5 minutes. Take out of oven and baste well. Give another 5 minutes, baste again and then add wine to the dish (champagne really is worthwhile) any remaining cream and cook for a further 30/40 minutes according to size. Baste at intervals. Test with a fork to see if flesh is tender. Taste for seasoning at this point, adjust if necessary, and stir sauce if necessary.

Meanwhile poach the cucumber cubes in salted water for 5 minutes. Do not let them lose their colour. Drain and keep hot. Cucumber cubes sautéd in butter is an alternative.

If serving from an oven dish, you can add the cucumber to the cream sauce. If not, decorate the serving dish with the cucumber, lift the fish out very carefully and spoon the sauce over fish and vegetable.

As fish come in all shapes and sizes, cooking times are very difficult to give. The times I give are guidelines only.

I'm sure it is quite unnecessary to add that champagne is the drink for this fish, and if it really is the fish of a life-time, then it must be worth it.

Salmon en Croûte

This recipe dates back to 1700, and can be used for any of the game fish, but it seems to suit the sea trout best, partly because of size. Salmon are too big and trout too small. You end up with more pastry than fish and there are so many other ways of dealing with them. So for this dish, I would use sea trout or grilse, and it's a memorable dish. Traditionally head and tail were left exposed rather like Star Gazey Pie.

Sea trout or grilse (ideally 3 lbs in weight)
1½ lb puff pastry (frozen will do)
2 oz butter
2 oz breadcrumbs soaked in milk
Sprigs of as many fresh herbs as possible
1 teaspoon of ground mace
¼ pint of thick cream
4–6 oz prawns or shrimps sautéd
1 lemon
Seasoning

Clean and gut fish, and for this recipe skin it. Put on one side and make pastry (if frozen pastry not used). This should be rolled out as thinly as possible, just a bit longer than the fish and about three times as wide. Leave to rest while making the stuffing.

Squeeze the breadcrumbs to get rid of surplus milk. Add the finely chopped herbs reserving 4 sprigs of the tarragon whole. Work in the butter and put in the salt, pepper and mace. Beat well. Stuff the cavity of the fish with this mixture. Place the fish in the middle of the puff pastry and brush the flesh with the double cream. Put sprigs of herbs on the cream. Sprinkle the fish with salt and pepper. Carefully fold the pastry round the fish. Either decorate with pastry fish shapes or make the join as decorative as possible. Press the pastry as tightly as can be round the fish. Place on baking tray and bake in a hot oven 400°F for the first 20 minutes. Reduce heat to 350°F and cook for a further 25–30 minutes. If getting too brown cover lightly with foil to prevent it becoming too dark, and if necessary place lower in the oven.

To serve, place on flat dish and decorate with the prawns lightly sautéd and the lemon cut in slices.

Salmon Pie

This dish comes from Scotland, and once again goes back to the time when salmon was so plentiful that no one would eat it without dolling it up. Those must have been the days!

2 lbs of cooked salmon (approximately)
1 lb puff pastry (frozen pastry will do)
1 lobster cooked and chopped
2 anchovies pounded or essence
4 hard boiled eggs
½ lb butter
4 glasses white wine (¼ pint)
Generous pinch of mace
Salt and pepper to taste
4 oz fish stock

Roll out pastry and let it rest while preparing the fish. Remove skin. Cut fish carefully into eight slices, keeping the shape of the fish if possible and arrange neatly in the bottom of well buttered pie dish. Quarter the hard boiled eggs, and place two quarters of the egg and a knob of butter between each slice of fish.

Put the remaining butter into a pan, melt and pour the white wine into it, stirring all the time. Add the fish stock, chopped lobster, anchovies (or essence), seasoning and mace. Pour this over the salmon. Cover with the pastry, decorate with a pastry fish if possible. Bake in a hot oven 400°F for at least 20 minutes. Lower temperature to 350°F and cook for another 15 minutes to ensure the salmon is heated thoroughly. Serve at once. Cut a slice of pastry out first, so that you can ensure that a complete slice of salmon can be given for each serving.

Small new potatoes and either petit pois or poached or sautéd cucumber cubes are all that this dish needs.

Baked Sea Trout

The sea trout is probably the most delicate flavoured of all game fish we have in this country, and so needs the simplest of treatment.

1 sea trout 3–4 lbs in weight
Fresh herbs, fennel, thyme, tarragon,
 chives, etc.
Seasoned flour
Butter

Butter a cooking dish and lay some of the herbs on the base. Clean the fish and pat dry, rub the seasoned flour all over the outside, season the inside and pop some more fresh herbs and a knob of butter in cavity. Lay in dish over the herbs, cover with buttered foil, and cook in a preheated oven 350°F for 30 minutes. Remove foil and cook for a further 10 minutes to crisp the flavoured skin.

This is ideal hot or cold, but if serving hot, pour juices over, and remove the herbs before serving. Excellent with browned almonds.

If served cold, lemon mayonnaise and fresh cucumber makes, we think, a very special dish.

Traditionally Hollandaise sauce is served with this beautiful fish. Personally, we rarely serve this in these cholesterol conscious days, but as it goes with a lot of fish, I have given a recipe for it among the sauces. We prefer a Lemon Sauce which seems to be a Scottish recipe.

Trout in Herb Cream

1 small trout per person
¼ pint milk
¼ pint cream
2 oz white breadcrumbs
3 oz butter
Sprigs of tarragon or fennel per fish
1 tablespoon of finely chopped mixed herbs (tarragon, chives, thyme, parsley, etc)
Seasoned flour

Clean trout, and rub over with the seasoned flour. Place in buttered dish, placing sprig of fresh herb inside each fish with a little knob of butter, from the given amount. Pour milk into dish, and cook in ready preheated oven, covering with foil or lid. Bake at 400°F for 20–30 minutes depending on size of fish. Take out of oven, add the chopped herbs to the cream, and stir into the cooking liquid. Sprinkle the breadcrumbs evenly over each fish, dot with the remaining butter. Place under a hot grill for long enough to brown the crumbs, and the cream to bubble.

Serve from cooking dish.

Small Trout in Lemon Jelly

4 small 'stockies' or brook trout
$\frac{1}{4}$ pint good dry wine
1 small onion finely chopped
1 bay leaf
1 small teaspoon of mixed herbs (thyme, tarragon, chives)
4 peppercorns
2 tablespoons finely chopped parsley
Rind and juice of large lemon
Sachet of gelatine
Butter for cooking
Salt to taste

Butter a baking dish and lay the trout in it. As these are small trout, leave heads and tails on, (merely gut and clean). Put wine, onion, bay leaf, peppercorns, herbs and thinly peeled lemon rind into a saucepan. Bring to the boil and simmer gently for 15 minutes. Strain this liquor and pour over the trout. Cover with lid or foil and put into a fairly hot oven 350°F for no more than 15–20 mins. When cooked, lift trout and remove skin. Place on attractive dish. Add lemon juice to the liquid the fish was cooked in, and stir in gelatine. Carefully pour the lemon jelly over the trout, and serve cold with crisp salad, brown bread and butter, and mayonnaise with a little lemon juice added.

If you want to decorate the trout for a special

party, brush trout with gelatine mix and fix ½ rounds of cucumber slices 'scale-like' before pouring over the main bulk of the jelly.

This is a continental recipe and we have friends who serve this with Danish lumpfish roe. This is cheap but does look expensive. In fact, its sold as caviare!

Garnish with the parsley.

Stuffed Trout Cooked in Vine Leaves

This was a favourite recipe of Toulouse-Lautrec, but he cooked his in a pit with a large stone over embers.

4 trout (1 lb or less)
½ lb butter
½ pint shrimps (cut in half)
Salt and pepper to taste
Pinch of mace
4 sprigs of either fresh tarragon or lemon thyme
Vine leaves for wrapping, well buttered and wiped over with lemon juice or wine vinegar.

Clean the trout well and gut. If you are expert at emptying the gut through the gills, this leaves a nice pocket for the stuffing to stay intact.

Place a sprig of herb in each fish. Mix butter, mace and shrimps together, season with the salt and pepper and divide into 4 portions. Place a portion in each fish. Squeeze any lemon juice over on the fish.

Wrap each trout in vine leaves covering completely. Secure with kitchen string. Place in an oven dish, buttered lightly. Cook in hot oven 375°F for ¾ hour, with either a foil covering, or lid.

Serve with crisp parsley, lemon slices and (ideally) really small new potatoes, well minted.

Our local delicatessen sells Greek vine leaves in brine. They are bigger than my English ones, but slightly tougher and they do need to be washed to get excess salt out.

If using fresh leaves, blanch in boiling water for 1–2 minutes.

Empingham Stuffed Trout

This is a great favourite of the local hostelry, and they do it beautifully. It does have a lovely surprise for the taste buds, and you may not have thought of doing it. Do try it.

Trout (under a lb if possible, 1 per person)
5 oz fresh bread crumbs
2 oz butter
1 tablespoon finely chopped parsley
1 teaspoon of mixed herbs
Grated rind of an orange
Segments of the orange roughly chopped, skin and pith removed
5 oz toasted and roughly chopped hazelnuts
1 large egg beaten
Grated rind of 1 lemon
Salt and pepper to taste
Butter for cooking

Clean and gut trout. Put all ingredients in a bowl and mix well. As breadcrumbs vary, a little more liquid may be needed, in which case fresh orange juice is added until the mixture binds lightly, not a soggy mess.

Divide the mixture equally between fish to be stuffed and stuff the cavity. Secure with wooden cocktail sticks if necessary. Lay the trout in well buttered dish, dot with butter, and season well. Cover with foil or lid and bake in a hot oven 375°F for 45 minutes at least, to ensure the stuffing is cooked.

Serve on a hot dish decorated with orange segments fresh parsley sprigs and small new potatoes, buttered and sprinkled with finely scissored chives.

Rutland Trout

This is a nice way of cooking the smaller trout.

4 trout
1 pint shelled prawns
¼ lb of butter
Tarragon or thyme
Seasoning

Make sure the fish are well cleaned, wipe dry. Divide the butter and prawns (or shrimps can be used) into 4 equal portions. Sprinkle the herb over each portion. and season. Carefully fill the cavity in each fish with the mixture and secure with cocktail sticks (wooden ones). Sprinkle each fish with a squeeze of lemon juice, wrap individually in buttered foil, and cook in hot oven 375°F for ½ hour.

If you are lucky enough to have a barbecue you can cook over hot embers for 20 minutes, turning once during cooking. It may be as well to double wrap the trout to ensure the juices don't escape during the cooking process.

There are barbecues at the Barnsdale end of Rutland Water and Normanton has some, which makes it very pleasurable for the angler's family to enjoy this dish after a good fishing session.

Sykes Lane Trout

Some of the trout are really large in Rutland Water, and these fish can be seen, dashing amongst the shoals of fry, especially if you haven't a rod handy. To me the following seems a very fitting recipe for such a fish, if you are able to catch one. My husband has been lucky enough to land a few.

1 large trout
1 glass of dry wine or cider
¼ lb butter with herbs and lemon juice
Seasoning
1 tablespoon of Anchovy essence (optional)
Whitebait
Seasoned flour
Oil for frying

Clean and gut trout. Make a maître d'hôtel butter, by beating herbs and lemon juice into the butter. Add anchovy essence if being used. Spread the butter generously over the inside of the fish, covering all the flesh. Put the fish into a well buttered ovenproof dish. Spread more of the butter over the skin, cover with foil, and bake in oven 375°F for 35–45 minutes depending on size. Put on a warm dish and keep hot.

Prepare whitebait, by shaking in a freezer bag with seasoned flour, and cook in hot oil in usual way.

Put whitebait round the dish with the trout in centre, and serve at once.

Garnish only with parsley and lemon slices. The juices the fish was cooked in can have a squeeze of lemon and 2 tablespoons of cream added, but serve in a sauceboat to keep whitebait crisp at time of serving.

Savoury Baked Trout

(A very good way of cooking out-of-condition fish)

This is an American recipe, and we may think twice about cooking salmon in this fashion, which they do. I understand the American salmon is not quite up to the standard of fish caught in this country. But if any trout is not quite in the pink (either it is too early in the season, or not the best water for some reason) this may be just the recipe to perk it up.

Fillets of trout up to 3 lbs
1 onion, chopped finely
½ green pepper, sliced
1 clove garlic crushed
½ lb chopped tomatoes
2 bay leaves, crumbled
4 rashers of bacon
Dash of Worcester sauce, to taste
Butter for frying

Fry the chopped onion in the butter. When just transparent throw in the pepper and garlic. When these have turned colour slightly, add the chopped tomatoes, and bay leaves. Cook for 5 minutes over heat. Add Worcester sauce.

Line a shallow dish with bacon rashers. Put the fish fillets on top of these neatly, then cover with the hot vegetables.

Bake in hot oven for 45 minutes.

Troute Rosé

This is an ideal recipe for trout out of the freezer or that are less than perfect. If they are not quite in the pink, by the time you have finished this recipe they should have a gentle blush. I have not tried this particular recipe on fish over 1½ lbs.

Trout—defrosted if necessary
Bottle of dry Rosé Anjou or a light dry red
3 Shallots finely chopped
Bay leaves
Sea Salt
Black pepper
Buffer for cooking and for sauce
2 or 3 cloves, optional
1 oz flour

When trout is defrosted, and 3–4 hours before cooking, butter an earthenware or glass cooking dish. Lay trout in it. If one trout only, pop 2 bay leaves in the cavity and season, or 1 bay leaf per small fish.

Chop shallots very finely and sprinkle over and around the trout. Cover with the Rosé or light red wine, season, and put in a cool place, turning fish over every hour.

Set oven to 350°F well before needed. Cover dish carefully with tight fitting lid or foil, and put in oven when hot. Timing will depend on size of fish. If small one of say ¾ lb give 25 to 30 minutes. A larger fish up to 1½ lbs will need 40 to 45 minutes.

When cooked, lift out carefully onto serving dish and keep hot.

For sauce, melt 1 oz of butter in pan, and stir in 1 oz of flour. When blended, pour in the wine the fish was cooked in, stirring all the time. Cook gently for 3 minutes, and if too thick add rosé wine until right consistency, heated right through. The sauce should have a faint blush.

Pour sauce over fish. Serve with creamed potatoes. As it is an autumn or even winter dish, try some tinned artichoke hearts, lightly sautéd in a little butter.

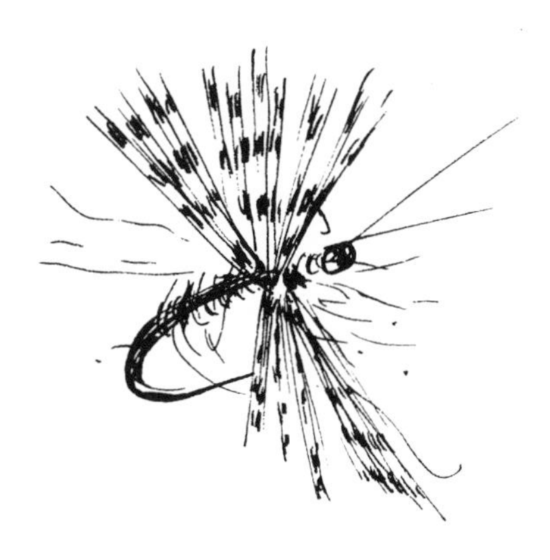

Whisky Trout

Although this recipe is American, I feel it was probably taken over there by migrating Scots. Small trout are best for this recipe.

4 trout (small ones preferably)
$\frac{1}{4}$ lb butter
Crushed clove garlic
Salt and pepper to taste
Chopped green onions 1 per fish
Chopped parsley (I use a lot)
1 tablespoonful grapeseed oil
1 large measure of whisky

Butter an oven dish evenly, and put aside. Mix oil, salt, pepper, and crushed garlic and brush this over the trout, both sides. Put into oven dish, and sprinkle with parsley and chopped onions. Dot with remaining butter. Pour whisky evenly over the fish. Cook in preheated oven 375°F for 30 minutes, basting at least twice during cooking time. To make sure fish is cooked, test with a fork.

This can also be done in a frying pan.

Serve with lemon slices.

Pickled Trout Fillets

This is a good recipe for dealing with a surplus of trout if the freezer is full. It is also useful because the trout will keep for sometime in a cool place.

Trout fillets
½ lb butter
¼ pint tarragon vinegar
A good pinch of each of the following, mace, nutmeg and cloves ground
Salt and pepper to taste

Clean fish in usual way and fillet. Pour over the tarragon vinegar, and sprinkle with salt and pepper. leave in a cool place for some hours. Then place fish top to tail in a buttered baking dish, cover with lid or foil, and bake in a slow oven 325°F for ¾ hour. When cool carefully lift out and place on a clean shallow dish. Meanwhile heat the remaining butter and while still liquid pour carefully over the trout fillets, ensuring they are completely covered. Do not use cooking juices.

Because trout has such a delicate flavour, I find a simple salad (crisp) is all that it needs to accompany this dish.

Trout Kedgeree

This lovely recipe was given to be by Marcus Warwick, well known for his superb rod making, but just as famous for his culinary skills and love of good food.

1½ lb trout poached in salt water
2 cups of cooked long grain rice
2 large onions
3 hard boiled eggs shelled
Butter for cooking
Seasoning

When trout is cool enough to handle, skin and remove bones and flake flesh. Put on one side.

Butter an oven proof dish 12″ × 8″ × 2″, and put a layer of sliced onion on the bottom. Cover this with a layer of the cooked rice, sprinkle half the trout on this covered by the finely chopped egg white, put flakes of butter on top of this and season with freshly ground pepper and salt.

Repeat layers, ending with the hard boiled yolks grated as the final layer. Season again and dot with butter.

Cover with greased proof paper, to ensure the rice does not harden. Cook in preheated oven 350°F for 30 minutes to cook onion and heat everything thoroughly.

Serve at once from dish. Chopped parsley is the only garnish needed as the layers make it a very attractive dish to serve.

Roast Stuffed Pike

Every fly-fisherman at sometime or another has caught a pike instead. Well, don't despair. It is delicious, and a highly thought of dish on the Continent. Toulouse-Lautrec had dozens of ways of cooking this fierce fish.

1 pike (anything over 5 lbs)
1 lb sausage meat
¼ lb breadcrumbs
Prawns
1 teaspoon of following herbs – thyme, tarragon, oregano
Salt and pepper to taste
½ lb sautéd pink mushrooms in 2 oz of butter
1 tablespoon Anchovy essence
Bacon rashers to cover pike during cooking
White wine for pouring over pike in dish

Clean fish very well, scale and pat dry.

In a big bowl mix all the ingredients, except wine and bacon, until evenly mixed. I've used pink mushrooms in this recipe because they do not go dark during the cooking, thus possibly spoiling the pink and white effect of this lovely dish. Fill the cavity carefully with the stuffing, and secure with cocktail sticks, or sew up if geared to that method.

Put the fish in a suitable baking tray, lay the bacon over the fish evenly. Pour enough good dry white wine to cover the bottom of the dish ¾ inch. Cover with oiled foil and cook in a medium oven 370°F, basting frequently during cooking. The time will depend on the size of the pike.

If the pike is much bigger you will have to juggle the stuffing to fit the fish. My measurements are for average fish.

Baked Grayling

I have to admit, it is years since I tasted grayling and I don't think I would even recognise it, if placed before me. However, it is highly thought of, and it is useful because it is good in winter, when other fish are not available. Grayling can be cooked as trout.

4 grayling
1 oz butter
Seasoned flour
Glass of Burgundy

Clean and gut fish, and remove scales.

Butter an ovenproof dish, Coat the fish in the seasoned flour and put a flake of butter on each grayling. Pour the wine over the fish and bake in a moderate oven 350°F, basting at least three times during cooking time. Allow 30 minutes.

Foil-baked Fish

(Especially Sea Trout and Grilse)

This is ideal for sea trout, with its very delicate flavour, or grilse. A perfect trout or salmon piece can also be cooked with this method.

1 sea trout or other weighing approx.
  3 lbs–5 lbs
Squeeze of lemon
Seasoning
1 oz butter
Oil for foil

Clean and gut fish, remove all blood from cavity, and brush inside with lemon juice. Flake the butter and spread evenly inside and season.

Have a large piece of foil (oiled) and place fish in the centre. Make a secure parcel by wrapping the fish and twisting the ends of the foil.

Although you don't want it to leak, it is better to have a loose parcel.

Place on baking tray and cook in preheated oven 375°F for 40–50 minutes, or longer according to its size.

Remove from oven and allow 15–20 minutes for fish to rest.

Open parcel carefully, and place fish on serving dish, when cool enough to handle.

If it is to be garnished, remove uppermost skin while still warm.

Trout in Orange Sauce

This is a dish for trout out of the freezer, or farmed trout, which after the beautiful fish anglers catch, seem very unattractive, and need some culinary titivation.

2 trout under 1 lb, or 1 large trout 1½ lb.
2 ozs butter
Sage, chives, and lemon thyme, or herbs of own choice
Seasoned flour
Rind of 2 large oranges and 5 ozs of juice
Breadcrumbs (about 2 ozs)
Butter for cooking

Clean and gut trout carefully, and wipe dry. Put the butter and breadcrumbs into a bowl and wipe oranges carefully, taking care not to release the zest. Then finely grate as much of the peel into the bowl as possible. Season the mix and add the very finely chopped herbs or dried herbs. Beat all together. Spread this mixture evenly into the cavity of the fish (if too dry, add a little fresh orange juice, enough to make a smooth, not liquid, paste).

Cut oranges in half and extract every bit of juice. Put fish into a well buttered dish, dredge lightly with seasoned flour, and pour orange juice over. Dot fish with flakes of butter.

Put into preheated oven, 350°F for 20 to 35 minutes according to size. Cover with lid of foil, but baste at least 3 times during cooking, the butter, flour and orange juice make a lovely sauce. Leave uncovered for the last 10 minutes. If the oranges did not have enough juice, add some unsweetened orange from a carton to make up to the required amount.

Serve with creamy potatoes and very fresh watercress.

4 Poaching Liquids and Methods

Various Poaching Liquids

General Purpose Court-bouillon

12 black peppercorns
4 cloves
bouquet garni (fish one if possible)
1 pint of dry white wine or dry cider
1 large carrot
1 large onion (not the sort to make your eyes water)
1 large leek
Sea salt to taste

Lightly crush peppercorns. Put herbs and spices in muslin. Coarsely cut up vegetables. Put all ingredients into pan to be used for fish, add 1 pint of water, bring all this to the boil, and then simmer gently for 30 minutes with the lid off. Allow to cool then taste for seasoning and adjust to taste.

The court-bouillon is now ready for poaching your fish. After the fish is cooked and removed, this liquid can be reduced by further simmering and used for sauces, and fish soups, which are so lovely and a meal in themselves, in which case go easy on the salt.

Simple Court-bouillon

8 black peppercorns
medium sized mild onion
5 oz dry white white or two tablespoons of wine or tarragon vinegar
lemon rind thinly peeled (optional)
Salt to taste
2 pints of water

Lightly crush peppercorns. Peel and finely slice onion. Put all ingredients into pan to be used for fish. Add the liquid and bring to the boil and simmer for 30 minutes with the lid off. Allow to cool and check seasoning.

This particular court-bouillon is probably better for fish that are not quite in the pink as it were, for example red salmon that have spent too long in fresh water, or the dark trout that have not yet recovered after spawning.

Brine

3 pints of water to
$\frac{3}{4}$ lb salt

Add the salt to the water. If you are lucky enough to be near the sea, and the water is not polluted, do use that, with less salt of course. Bring to the boil and simmer for 20 minutes at least. Allow to cool before putting the fish in. Now brine is for the really superb salmon or trout that are lovely to look at, fat and silvery, and need nothing in the way of embellishments to improve them.

General Notes on Poaching without a Kettle

All the poaching liquids for game fish must be cool when the fish are put into the kettle, or pan.

If you do not possess a fish kettle, a very large

roasting tin can be used, with the court-bouillon of your choice, in the oven. The tin must be very well sealed with foil during cooking time.

Preheat oven to 325°F (slow) and allow 15 minutes per lb of fish. This does allow an attractive fish to be cooked whole for special occasions, rather than chopping it into portions. Treat the poached fish in exactly the same way as if it had been in a kettle. After testing for flakiness, turn oven off at once, and if possible remove pan from oven and place in cool place until almost cold, cooling the fish in its own liquor. If pan is so heavy and full it would be tricky to get out without accident, leave door ajar and allow fish to cool in its own liquor in the oven.

To Poach a Salmon, Sea Trout or Trout

The Scots understandably have a way with cooking their native fish, and no doubt it would make all followers of Mrs. Beeton turn pale at the simplicity of it all. However, if you have the courage to try out this recipe you will wonder what all the fuss was about. The first and most important thing is to catch your fish, which is the one thing that ensures it is the best fish you have ever eaten.

1 Salmon cleaned and gutted, any size as long as it fits into kettle
Bouquet garni
White wine (dry) bottle
Celery stalk chopped
2/3 carrots chopped
1 onion sliced
3 bay leaves
Blade of mace
Few peppercorns lightly crushed
Salt to taste

Put the fish into the kettle. Pour the bottle of wine over first, then top up with cold water, to ensure the fish is covered with liquid. Throw in the chopped vegetables and spices. Bring the contents to the boil and then simmer for three minutes. Remove from the heat at once and allow to cool naturally. Lift fish out carefully when cold, remove skin leaving head and tail intact. Garnish as required.

. . . .

If the fish is to be eaten hot, for the initial cooking a 6/7 lb fish will need to simmer for about 20 minutes, then be removed immediately from liquid and served. But as fish come in all sizes it is a problem to know exactly for how long to cook them. The fork test is probably the best way of telling when they are done.

If you are lucky enough to have landed something akin to the Loch Ness Monster I fear the only way to do it justice is to leave the tail end for poaching, and use the rest for cutting into steaks or stuffing.

Experiment with as many recipes as possible.

Tweed Kettle Salmon

This was a famous nineteenth century Edinburgh speciality, when salmon were almost two a penny, and workers didn't want them too often in their diet.

3 lbs of tail-end salmon (fresh)
2 tablespoons of chopped chives
½ pint fish stock
½ pint white wine
Pinch of ground mace
Salt and pepper to taste
2 tablespoons chopped parsley

Put the fish into a pan and cover with water. Bring to the boil and simmer for 5 minutes. Take off heat and remove the fish, but keep the water it was cooked in.

Skin the fish, and remove the bones. Cut the fish into cubes of two inches. Season with salt, pepper and mace. Put into pan with the fish stock, wine and chives.

Cover the pan tightly and simmer very slowly for 30 minutes. This dish can be served either hot or cold. As these quantities make enough for 5/6 portions it can be served cold next day. Add the chopped parsley just before serving either hot or cold.

Trout in Aspic

6 trout fillets (1 per person)
1 teaspoon salt
Water for cooking
1 onion peeled and finely sliced
2 bay leaves
2 tablespoons wine vinegar or lemon juice
6 peppercorns
Sachet of gelatine or aspic crystals
½ pint of cooked shrimps
2–3 hardboiled eggs (sliced)
¾ lb cooked peas as green as possible
(petit pois barely cooked are excellent)

Fillet the trout carefully. Roll up and secure with wooden cocktail sticks. Place in pan and cover with water. Add the onion, peppercorns, bay leaves, and lemon juice or vinegar. Bring to the boil and gently poach for 4–5 minutes, no more. Take out of pan carefully, so as not to break. Strain and reserve the liquid the fish were cooked in. Taste to see if more lemon juice or vinegar is needed. Dissolve aspic or gelatine in hot water as described on sachet and add to the fish liquid. If using aspic crystals the salt should be either omitted or reduced as aspic is already salted. Have a 3 pint ring mould or suitable cake tin, rinse it in cold water, set a few shrimps attractively over the bottom, cover with a thin layer of aspic, put in a cool place to set. When ready remove the cocktail sticks from the fillets and arrange on top of shrimps, with the egg slices, as neatly and attractively as possible. Put remaining shrimps on top of this with the peas. Cover with remaining aspic.

Gelatine is really better than aspic which has a strong flavour and can spoil the delicate flavour of the trout.

Chill for 2 hours at least before serving.

Truite au bleu

I am a little reluctant to give this recipe but it is so very famous that I have little choice!

Have ready a pan of boiling water (4 pints) and add ½ a pint of white wine vinegar. The trout should traditionally be thrown in whilst still alive, but good anglers always kill their fish as soon as they have landed them. However, the slime must still be on them, so do not rinse after gutting them. Remove any blood by rubbing salt onto them. Add a small handful of salt into the boiling water and carefully slip the trout in and simmer for 8–10 minutes according to size. It is the slime that gives this dish its name.

Serve with some parsley butter to which lemon juice has been added. Place this over the fish making sure they are evenly covered.

If you wish to serve this dish cold, after adding the fish to the pan bring the water back to the boil, and simmer for 3 minutes only. Remove pan from the heat and leave fish in the water to cool.

A very good sauce to serve with the cold version is as follows:

Horseradish Cream

Escoffier was very fond of horseradish with trout, so was Isaac Walton's friend Charles Cotton.

Take a pint of thick whipped cream. Add a tablespoon of strong horseradish sauce, one teaspoon of finely grated fresh ginger and the grated rind of a large lemon. If preferred use sour cream, which is excellent, instead of double cream; or according to the state of the larder, ½ cream and ½ mayonnaise. As for mayonnaise, if not homemade then the pale version on the grocer's shelf seems to be the very best for any game fish recipes.

5 Grilling and Frying

Scotch Breakfast Salmon

This is a very old recipe, which my grandfather used to tell me about, although at that time I had never even seen a salmon. I think it dates from a time when salmon were so commonplace, they had them for nearly every meal. If you are on a fishing holiday and self-catering, then this is a lovely way to start yet another fishing day, full of yesterday's salmon.

Salmon steaks with skin on
Beaten egg
Oatmeal
Butter for frying
No seasoning traditionally

Wipe the steaks and dip in the beaten egg. Have the oatmeal on a plate. Dip the egged steaks into the meal making sure the egged sides are well covered. Heat the butter in the pan. When bubbling (but not brown) put steaks into pan and cook for 10 to 12 minutes according to thickness. Turn once.

Traditionally these were not to be seasoned or have any fancy sauce with them. However, as with grilled salmon steaks, you may prefer a squeeze of lemon, but I am not sure that does anything for the oatmeal.

Small trout from the burn can be cooked in a similar way, and larger trout can be filletted and also cooked in the same way; and a very good meal it is too.

Grilled Fresh Salmon Steaks

We were given this simply delicious dish by a very sweet Scots woman. It was ready so quickly it didn't seem true but for good fish there is no need to tart it up. The salmon we ate was literally caught just minutes before. Mr. McCulloch, a very keen fisherman, who had a hot line to all likely points on the Cree and Minnoch, certainly caught his share of fish. His rod was always at the ready in the barn, and he would take off at the drop of a hat.

Salmon steaks one inch thick
Salt and pepper to taste
Melted butter for brushing over the steaks
Serve with lemon and parsley butter

Heat the grill on high for 2–3 minutes before grilling salmon. Brush the cutlets with melted butter, season to taste. Always use freshly ground pepper, really game fish is worth the extra trouble. Cook the salmon under the hot grill for 3–4 minutes only each side, brushing the underneath side and seasoning before putting back under the grill.

We ate ours with just a squeeze of lemon, but it is worth preparing some parsley butter if it is for a dinner party.

Trout with Almonds

I almost hesitate to give this recipe. It is so often served in rather mediocre restaurants, but cooked at home it is a pleasant dish and certainly very easy and quick.

4 trout (small ones are quite good for this recipe)
4 oz butter
4 oz almonds flaked
Seasoned flour
Lemon juice

Wash and clean the trout, pat dry. Rub all over with the flour until coated. Heat the butter in the pan until it is bubbling and fry the trout 4–5 minutes on each side. When ready put on a dish to keep hot. Add more butter to the pan if necessary and fry almonds until golden brown, no more.

Cover the fish evenly with the almonds and keep warm. Add the juice of a large lemon to the butter the fish and the almonds were cooked in and just bring to the boil. Pour over the fish at once.

Serve on a dish garnished with fresh parsley.

The nice thing about fried trout is that the skin is so delicious and it is a sin not to eat it, crispy and golden. Who can resist it (not too many fly-fishermen).

Savoury Trout

This is a quickie also, excellent for self catering on holiday.

Trout fillets
Packet of lemon and thyme stuffing
Butter or oil for frying
Beaten egg

Wipe fillets and dip in egg and then into the stuffing mix. Shake off surplus. Fry in hot oil or butter, turning once, for a few minutes.

If camping this is lovely eaten with the fingers.

Grilled Trout

This is another Marcus Warwick recipe, so easy to do and yet so lovely to eat.

One ¾ lb trout per person
Butter for cooking
2 tablespoons of best oil
2 tablespoons lemon juice
Salt and pepper

Scale, clean and gut trout. It is the scales that sometimes can carry the muddy flavour. Take rack out of grill pan as it is not used for this recipe.

Heat oil and a knob of butter in the bottom of the grill pan. When hot put the trout in, and immediately place a flake of butter on each fish and season. Place under grill and baste well. After 5 minutes, turn fish over in grill pan and return to heat, adding the lemon juice at this stage. Continue basting until fish is done (that is, a fork will ease flesh). The skin should be nice and crispy.

Serve at once, using the pan juices as a sauce.

Barnsdale Trout

After a hard days fishing, this recipe is easy, but has a touch of luxury that is not too taxing.

2 good sized trout fillets
$\frac{1}{2}$ lb pink mushrooms sliced
Butter for cooking
1 teaspoon of tarragon
1 glass of good dry wine, or tarragon vinegar diluted
4 tablespoons of cream
Salt and pepper to taste

Heat the butter in a thick frying pan, and when bubbling but not brown add the sliced mushrooms. Fry until cooked. Keep these warm. Flour the trout fillets, remove excess flour, and fry, skin side uppermost first, 4–5 minutes each side. When turned to expose pink fleshed underside, sprinkle the tarragon over the fillets, salt and pepper, pour over the glass of wine or diluted vinegar and cook gently until butter and wine have mingled. Now add mushrooms and cook for a further minute. Add cream just before serving, making sure it is well mixed with pan juices. Don't let it boil.

This can be served straight from the pan, otherwise transfer to warmed dish. We like this with just new potatoes, and mangetout peas if you have time to do them. These peas are very quick and easy. Top and tail, put a knob of butter in pan (or woks are ideal for these vegetables) and stir fry over high heat for 3 minutes. The peas should be brightly coloured and crisp.

Peking Trout

This recipe is for people like my son, who thinks he does not like fish, but will quite happily eat it from a Chinese 'take away'. I think one of the main reasons such people are wary of fish, is really that the bones bother them.

Which is why they will quite happily tuck into prawns but avoid fish. Also some people are sure that all trout have a muddy taste. This is to convince them that it really is otherwise.

Trout fillets very carefully boned
Sesame seeds (toasted) or rolled oats
Sweet and sour sauce (I buy a bottle)
Oil for frying
1 beaten egg seasoned
Dash of sesame oil

The last time I did this recipe it was with one of the large well-coloured fish my husband had caught at Rutland Water, but you can't always be that lucky with your catch. So the number of fillets used will depend on the fish of the moment. Cut the fillets into cubes (mine were about 2 inches square). Wipe the fillets and dip into the beaten egg, then press into the sesame seeds or rolled oats. Put these on one side and attend to the pan. Cover the base of a frying pan with a good oil. Excellent is the grapeseed oil, which is very fine. It has a very good nutty flavour and is high in polyunsaturates and vitamin E and low on cholesterol. It is well worth searching for. Although my local grocer stocks it, I have not seen it elsewhere. To this I add a tablespoon of sesame oil, for flavour. When the oil is hot put the cubes of fish carefully into the hot fat and fry for 3/4 minutes per side. They do not take long. If you make your own sweet and sour sauce do this before cooking the trout. If ready made sauce is used, heat it whilst cooking the fish.

Put crispy fish pieces on serving plate and cover with the heated sauce. Serve at once. This is more filling than would at first appear. I think although it looks like a starter, it does very well as a main course, especially with rice of your choice.

Trout in Oatmeal

Lovely way of cooking the little wild trout found in Scotland's lochs and burns.

2 small trout per person
Coarse oatmeal
Butter for frying
Salt and pepper
Diced bacon, 1 rasher per brace of fish (optional)

Clean the trout, slit open and remove backbone. Season the oatmeal with salt and pepper, then coat the fish, covering all over with the meal.

If bacon is to be used, fry diced bacon until slightly crisp. Remove from pan and keep warm. Heat the butter in the pan, mixing in with bacon fat. When bubbling but not brown, put in the trout. Cook on both sides until golden brown.

Serve with parsley and diced bacon, or lemon wedges if the bacon is not required.

This is my favourite breakfast when on holiday in Scotland. My husband catches and cooks the fish. Those wild trout with big eyes, they put up such a fight they deserve the best.

Jamaican Trout

Bananas are very versatile fruit and if you find yourself with some nice trout and very little else, just use what you have in the fruit bowl.

Trout fillets
Bananas
Butter for cooking
Lemon juice
Seasoning
Grapes for garnish
Coconut or sesame seeds

Wash and clean the trout, and fillet them. Squeeze some lemon juice over them and season. Peel the bananas and cut in half lengthwise, and half again lengthwise. Brush with lemon juice.

Heat butter in thick frying pan. When bubbling, pop in the fillets, skinside uppermost, and cook 4–5 minutes each side.

Place the fish on a warm serving dish and keep hot. Add more butter to the pan if necessary and quickly fry the banana slices. Place them equally over the fillets.

Sprinkle with either coconut or sesame seed. Add lemon juice to juices in the pan, and bring to the boil. Pour this over the fish.

Garnish with grapes. Serve with fluffy mashed potatoes.

Wiltshire Grayling

As grayling are probably eaten more in winter when trout are out of season, try cooking them with hazelnuts.

4 small grayling
3 oz hazelnuts chopped
Juice of 1 lemon
½ oz of butter
Seasoned flour
Grapeseed oil for frying

Clean and gut grayling. Remove Scales. Coat with the seasoned flour. Heat oil in thick frying pan and when hot, cook grayling 4–5 minutes each side. Transfer to a warm serving dish and keep hot.

Put the butter and lemon juice in the frying pan. When bubbling add the chopped nuts, turn them till brown. Don't let the butter burn. Pour over fish.

Serve with creamy potatoes.

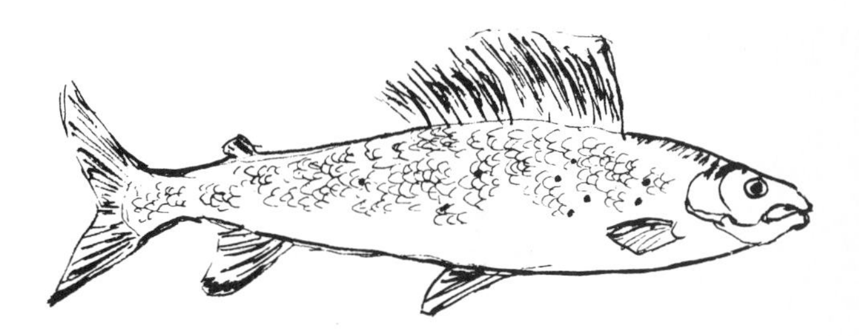

6 Sauces and Dressings

Prime fish need only the most simple of sauces to partner them but others do need some enhancement, and as you can do very little about the fish you can do everything about the accompaniments. I am only giving more unusual sauces here, but the scope is endless. Many books give recipes for everyday sauces.

Cream Sauce with Cucumber

½ pint of double cream
2 tablespoons of mayonnaise (white)
Grated cucumber, as much or as little as you need
Seasoning to taste
Dash of lemon juice, optional but nice

Whip the cream up and fold in mayonnaise. Leave the rind on the cucumber and grate on coarse side of grater. Add this to the cream mix. Add seasoning to taste and fold in lemon juice if being used. Serve at once.

In these days when cholesterol has to be thought about, the above recipe can be made using sour cream and is just as nice. The sharpness adds a refreshing taste to the fish.

Another excellent sauce for a prime fish is one using Caviare. Although easy to make it does add a touch of luxury and makes the angler justly proud of his catch.

Caviare Sauce

½ pint of Hollandaise sauce
4 oz double cream (whipped)
4 tablespoons of red caviare or
2 jars of red lumpfish roe (the latter is what we use)
Seasoning to taste.

Fold the cream into the ready made Hollandaise sauce and add the caviare just before serving. Taste, and adjust seasoning. Serve at once.

Parsley and Lemon Butter

Parsley and lemon butter is well worth making, when the parsley is at its best and freezing until needed.

Soften half a pound of butter, add the grated rind of a large lemon and all the juice and as much finely chopped parsley as you can incorporate. Beat well.

Taste before putting in freezer. Remember even the dullest grilled fish can be cheered up by the simplest means, and look very attractive too. To freeze this butter, I just roll it in portions of foil in the size that I will need for a family meal. It quickly softens at room temperature and a slice per serving is all that is needed.

Butter Sauce with Lemon, Fennel or Parsley Variations

This is a Scottish recipe from the 1700's. It is nice to make and will go with any fish. It is also good with vegetables. The thing about all these sauces is that you can vary them from time to time according to what is at hand.

I have given enough ingredients for 6/8 people, so if it is not all needed you can freeze the remainder for some other time, adding herbs or lemon as required.

8 oz butter
2 oz flour
¼ pint boiling salted water
1 egg yolk beaten with a tablespoon of cold water

Melt half the butter in a pan, and stir in the flour. When blended add the boiling salted water and beat or whisk well. Add the beaten egg yolk, but keep the mixture off the boil, stirring all the time. The remaining butter is then cut into nut size pieces. Drop these into the sauce 2/3 at a time, just keeping the pan off the heat to prevent boiling, beating well between additions.

To make lemon sauce add 1 tablespoon of lemon juice at this point.

Fennel is good with fish so you can reduce lemon juice and add finely chopped fennel for your taste.

Parsley sauce is very good made this way. Just taste to see how much lemon if any you need, and add as much parsley as you can use. The lovely green goes so well with the flesh colour of game fish, even before it gets to the taste buds.

Sauce Béchamel

This is a very traditional sauce and has been used for fish for centuries.

2 ozs butter
3 tablespoons flour
1 pint of milk
1 bay leaf
Seasoning

Heat the milk in a pan very slowly (with the bayleaf, to extract the full flavour) to just below boiling point.

Melt butter in another pan and stir in the flour, and cook without colouring for 2 minutes.

Take pan off the heat and gradually add the hot milk, beating well all the time, until it is all added. Simmer sauce gently, for 15–20 minutes, stirring regularly. If you are too busy to stand and stir, place saucepan over a pan of simmering water and stir occasionally.

The sauce will be reduced, and be of creamy texture.

To this you can either add herbs of your choice, eggs, or fish, whatever your needs are for the fish you are cooking.

A meagre portion of cream added, and a dash of lemon juice or sherry, is gorgeous with game fish.

Piquant Sauce

This sauce is excellent with all fish, but especially with pike. I use more butter than for normal sauces.

1 tablespoon flour
3 oz butter
5 oz good dry wine
5 oz fish stock (use ½ fish stock cube if no bits available)
1 onion finely chopped
1 clove garlic
1 dessertspoon tarragon
1 teaspoon mace
Lemon juice from 1 lemon or dash of tarragon or wine vinegar
Salt and pepper to taste

Cook the onion, garlic and herbs in the butter, until transparent. Sprinkle the flour and mix in: don't let it get brown. Add the liquid, stirring well. Don't let the sauce boil. Just simmer for 3 minutes, stirring all the time.

Hollandaise Sauce

This is a traditional sauce and originally came from Holland and was known as Dutch sauce. It is a very good basic recipe to which you can add finely chopped herbs of your choice, or which you happen to have in profusion. Bear in mind that herbs do compliment and bring out the best flavour of any fish (game or otherwise).

It is an easy sauce to make, but a little care is needed because to let it boil is a disaster. The beauty of it is the velvety texture, like a good hot mayonnaise.

3 tablespoons white wine vinegar
2 tablespoons water, if necessary
3 egg yolks
½ lb butter, soft and lightly beaten
Seasoning
Squeeze of lemon juice

Boil vinegar in a pan to reduce its quantity to about 1 tablespoon. Cool slightly, add a knob of butter and, still off the heat, add the well beaten egg yolks. Stand the pan or bowl being used in a saucepan of boiling water. Stir, with a wooden spoon. As the sauce begins to thicken, add the butter a little at a time stirring all the time. If the sauce should be too thick after all the butter has been added, the cold water may be added until the right creamy consistency is obtained. The sauce should coat the back of the spoon. To keep hot, leave over barely simmering water until ready to use. Season and add squeeze of lemon juice.

Tasty Sauce for Trout, or any Freshwater Fish

¼ pint Hollandaise sauce (see recipe above)
3 tablespoons fish stock (stock cube if necessary)
2 tablespoons of finely grated raw carrots
1 tablespoon of finely chopped raw parsley
1 teaspoon of finely grated fresh ginger (the powdered will not do)
The grated rind of a small orange
2 glasses of dry white wine
Seasoning

Add the grated vegetables to a pan. Pour on the wine and bring to boil. Boil until the wine is just about absorbed. Pour on the fish stock and bring to the boil again. When there is only a spoonful of liquid left, allow to cool slightly (Hollandaise sauce must never boil). Add the Hollandaise sauce and stir into the vegetables, ensuring the liquid in the pan is well mixed in. Just before serving, heat the sauce almost to boiling point and then pour into sauce boat.

Sherry Sauce

This is one of my favourites, and we use dry sherry. However, use the sherry you normally drink, otherwise it may be too dry for you. Just add 2 tablespoons of sherry and the juice of one lemon to cream sauce, omitting the cucumber.

Dill Mayonnaise

2 tablespoons of French mustard
1 large egg yolk
1 pint Flora, sunflower oil, or corn oil
2 tablespoons white wine vinegar
Salt and pepper to taste
Teaspoon of dill

Beat the mustard and egg yolk together, then drip oil very slowly into the mixture, beating all the time until it thickens. When oil is all incorporated add the dill and seasoning.

This mayonnaise is very good with salmon.

Mayonnaise for Chaud-froid

This is a very good covering instead of aspic, especially if the fish is pale.

Make mayonnaise up in usual way, as described above, or ready prepared will do well, if it is a good pale coloured one. To about 1 pint of mayonnaise fold in gently ¼ pint of firm aspic or even gelatine on the point of setting. It must be poured on the fish before it sets so the fish should be cold.

Green Mayonnaise

½ pint of good mayonnaise
2 hardboiled eggs
2 green onions finely chopped
4 oz of four green herbs (tarragon, chives, sorrel, parsley, chervil or borage)
Salt and pepper
Grated lemon rind and juice
3 tablespoons of yoghourt or sour cream

Grate lemon rind and add the juice. Chop herbs and onion very finely, and add to mayonnaise with the lemon.

Do the same with eggs. Season to taste and add the sour cream or yoghourt. This is good with any poached fish being served cold. Tarragon vinegar can be used instead of lemon juice.

English Sauce (Lemon Sauce)

I prefer this sauce to the Hollandaise which is so full of cholesterol. Although there is no substitute for butter, I do try to keep the amount used as low as possible, unlike Mrs. Beeton, who used it by the ton.

6 oz butter
1 oz flour
¼ pint boiling salted water
1 egg yolk beaten in tablespoon cold water
1 dessertspoon lemon juice or more

Melt half the butter in pan and stir in the flour. Add the boiling salted water and beat well. Take it off the heat and beat in the beaten egg yolk. Stand the pan in another one of boiling water. Add the remaining butter in small knobs, beating all the time, and on no account let the mixture boil. Stir in the lemon juice, to taste. I like mine really sharp. Because all the fish in this book are quite fatty, the acid helps to counteract this.

Caviare and Cucumber Sauce

If you have a good fish and simply want to poach or bake it to have cold with a salad, this is a pretty sauce.

Carton of sour cream
Grated or finely diced cucumber
Juice and grated rind of 1 lemon
½ jar of red lumpfish roe or caviare
2 tablespoons of Hellmann's pale mayonnaise
Seasoning to taste

Grate or dice cucumber. I grate mine into a fine sieve and leave standing on kitchen paper, shaking from time to time to get out excess moisture.

Put all the ingredients into a bowl and taste for seasoning last of all. This sauce has a lovely pink look, and the cucumber crispness goes well with the delicate taste and texture of the trout.

Shrimp Sauce

This is a delicate sauce and is very good to serve with trout that is very pale. The shrimps add the necessary colour, without spoiling the flavour.

1 tablespoonful flour
2 oz butter
½ pint stock (fish cube or court-bouillon)
5 oz dry white wine
½ pint of shelled shrimps
Salt and pepper to taste
Tomato ketchup (not for taste, just a faint blush, optional)
Mace (a good pinch)

Melt butter in saucepan. Sprinkle flour over and mix in, stirring all the time. Gradually add the liquid. Simmer for 2 minutes. Add shrimps, seasoning, mace and just a soupçon of tomato ketchup if a delicate colour is needed. Bring up to simmering point before serving.

Fresh Ginger Sauce

For a poached trout/salmon you wish to serve cold. Cold sauces are easy to prepare, and we find sour cream doesn't detract from the fish. Strong mayonnaise can overpower the delicate flavour completely.

The green of the fruit shows the pink flesh off very well.

Carton of sour cream
1 Kiwi fruit
Fresh grated ginger (heaped teaspoonful)
Squeeze of lemon/lime juice
Seasoning to taste

Peel and dice the kiwi fruit. Put into a bowl and mix with the other ingredients and serve cold.

The amount of grated ginger depends entirely on individual palates.

Basic low-cholesterol sauce

A basic sauce of 1 oz flour and 1 oz butter can be used instead of the more traditional ones high in cholesterol. To the flour and butter just add the wine stock or cooking liquid instead of the milk normally used. If a really creamy sauce is needed, just add a dash of cream at the last moment. Add herbs or prawns or whatever else you decide on. Half of one fish stock cube gives a good flavour, but check before adding.

7 Starters, Quickies and Smoked Fish Dishes

Party Pieces

If it is your own smoked salmon, use all the odd bits and pieces, other than the prime side, otherwise buy cheaper pieces for all of these recipes.

Smoked Salmon Balls

1 lb smoked salmon pieces finely minced or blended
½ lb butter
juice of ½ lemon
seasoning
pepper, freshly ground
Finely chopped mixed nuts, Toasted sesame seeds, Crushed garlic croutons } coatings
Stuffed green olives and parsley for garnish

Mix salmon, butter, lemon juice and black pepper together in a bowl. Test for salt, add if necessary. Keep cool, and form into small balls. Put the coatings into separate bowls. Divide the balls into three lots and roll in these coatings. Cover with seeds, nuts and croûtons. Pile onto an attractive plate and garnish with drained olives and parsley, pyramid fashion.

Smoked Salmon Tarts

24 baked pastry cases
8 oz smoked salmon pieces
4 oz butter
2 tablespoons best mayonnaise (Hellmann's)
2 tablespoons sour cream
juice of a lemon
lemon slices
Pinch of cayenne
Seasoning
Parsley sprigs

Blend the salmon and butter together, then beat in lightly the sour cream, mayonnaise and lastly the lemon juice. Taste before adding salt and use freshly ground pepper. Fill each case with mixture. Cut lemon slices and place on each tart before serving. Sprinkle very lightly with a pinch of cayenne over the tarts – just a whisper. Add a sprig of parsley on each tart.

General Notes

Asparagus is a very good companion for fresh or smoked salmon, but the tinned variety of asparagus is so mushy and dull in colour, I think it is only worth using the fresh.

Smoked salmon wrapped round fresh barely cooked asparagus tips is memorable, even if it is a once a year treat.

Green grapes and stoned black olives (the large ones) with diced salmon pieces with an oil and wine vinegar dressing on crisp lettuce is very good.

Best smoked salmon ideally needs only brown bread and butter, lemon juice and freshly ground black pepper. In fact, incorporating the lemon juice into the butter before making sandwiches is easier than squeezing lemon juice on afterwards.

Pieces of less prime fish need a little titivation. Fresh fruit such as melon or grapefruit cut into small pieces, mixed with neat slivers of smoked salmon, tossed into a good dressing, with wine, or wine vinegar, not malt vinegar, and served on a bed of Iceberg or Webb's lettuce, fresh and crisp, is a very good starter for a rich main course.

Alternatively, try cucumber cut into small neat cubes, sprinkled with lemon or fresh lime juice, wrapped in a small slice of smoked salmon, secured with a cocktail stick, served with large black olives.

Smoked Trout/Salmon Cheesecake

4 oz water biscuits, crushed
2 oz butter, softened
8 oz smoked trout or salmon pieces
1 lb Philadelphia or cream cheese
3 large eggs
1 sachet gelatine
½ pint sour cream
1 lemon (grated rind and juice)
Fresh ginger finely grated to taste
Seasoning
3 oz hot water

Dissolve gelatine in water. Melt the butter, add to the crushed biscuits, and line the bottom of a loose bottomed 8 inch cake tin. Put aside to cool. Separate the eggs and beat the yolks into the cream cheese. Grate the lemon and extract the juice. Add these to the cheese mix.

Finely dice the smoked fish, keeping a few pieces for garnishing. Whip the egg whites and fold into the cheese mix together with the fish, ginger and dissolved gelatine. Season to taste.

Pour into cake tin and leave in a cool place to set. When ready remove the base from tin and leave cake on the base. Garnish with the reserved pieces of fish, cucumber and parsley.

This is a lovely buffet dish and the addition of the fresh ginger does add a piquancy. This is a very old idea. Isaac Walton's friend Cotton used it a lot in his fish cooking.

I think we are turning more to traditional tastes and cooking methods.

Smoked Salmon Eclairs

Small baked éclairs
4 oz smoked salmon pieces
4 oz Philadelphia or cream cheese
Black pepper freshly ground
Salt if needed
Small glass of dry sherry
Parsley for garnish

Chop salmon pieces very finely and beat into cream cheese. Add black pepper to taste. Add sherry until mixture is nice and creamy. Fill éclair cases (leave till just before serving, to stop them going soggy). Garnish with fresh parsley sprigs.

This filling will also do for putting into pastry cases. The sherry can be replaced by dry wine or fresh lemon/lime juice, but it is lovely with sherry.

The variations are endless. It is worth experimenting, but do use the best ingredients, fruit or vegetables, as fresh as possible.

Smoked Salmon and Avocado

¼ lb smoked salmon trimmings will do
2 good avocados (no dark bits)
2 tablespoons sour cream
2 tablespoons white mayonnaise
Juice of a lemon
Seasoning to taste

Cut smoked salmon into small even sized pieces. Mix the sour cream and mayonnaise together, add the salmon. Season to taste. Keep cool.

Make sure the avocados are ripe, but don't prepare until ready for the meal. Cut fruit in half, remove stones and brush the cut surfaces with the lemon juice.

Pile salmon mix on top, garnish with finely chopped parsley.

Caviare and Trout or Salmon Starter

This is a very versatile dish. It seems to go equally well with fresh trout and salmon, or smoked, so do ring the changes.

Carton of sour cream
Red lumpfish roe (1 jar) or caviare
Juice and rind of 1 lemon
Cold fish (fresh or smoked pieces will do)
1 tablespoon of Hellmann mayonnaise
Season to taste
Iceberg or Webbs lettuce, shredded

Mix the sour cream and lumpfish roe or caviare. Reserve a spoonful of the roe for garnish. Add grated rind and juice of lemon, mayonnaise, and either flaked cold fish, or smoked fish cut into pieces. Season to taste and chill.

Just before serving arrange crisp lettuce into serving glasses and top with the fish mix. Put a few grains of roe on top of each serving. Serve with wafer thin brown bread and lemon butter.

This also makes a nice dip for all the green fresh vegetables available, cucumber strips, celery, peppers sliced, carrots.

We also like it piled onto avocados.

If sour cream is difficult to get, use cream cheese, or Philadelphia, but you may need more lemon juice.

Smoked Salmon Quiche

If you have only scraps of smoked salmon or trout left, and you want to stretch them to feed a family, this quiche is very tasty and filling. It is nice enough to offer guests.

1 cooked pastry case
¼ lb scraps of smoked fish (the more the better, obviously)
½ pint cream
3 egg yolks
Salt and pepper to taste
Mace powdered
Anchovy essence (if smoked fish very sparse)
Cayenne pepper few grains
Fresh parsley finely chopped (or tarragon)
Any cold fish (trout or salmon best) if available for extra filling

Cut the smoked fish into even sized pieces (thumb-nail size). Beat the egg yolks and add to the cream. Season to taste with salt, pepper and mace. Add the anchovy essence if being used. Mix in the herbs and the smoked fish and any cooked fish. Pour into the pastry case, making sure the fish is evenly distributed. Bake in a moderately hot oven 350°F for about 45 minutes or until cooked. Sprinkle with cayenne.

Alternatively, you can use small pastry cases. Cooking time for these tartlets is 30 minutes at the same temperature as above.

Small new potatoes, well buttered, sprinkled with either chopped parsley or scissored chives are ideal to serve with the quiche. A very simple side salad with a good crisp lettuce like Webbs or Iceberg, is really all that is needed, unless you have some tender asparagus which is even better.

Smoked Salmon Marinated with Dill

If the smoked salmon is a prime fish this is a waste, but for a mediocre one this is a way of making the most of it.

½ lb of smoked salmon
Small teaspoon of dill seeds
1 teaspoon of peppercorns
1 tablespoon chopped chives
¼ pint of good dry white wine
Bay leaf
Salt to taste
Lemon juice from large lemon

Put the fish in glass dish (not metal), sprinkle with peppers and dill seed, crumble bay leaf and add. Cover with white wine and place in fridge or cool place over night. Just before serving drain the wine and spices off of the salmon. Put half of the wine into a bowl, add the cream, season to taste with salt, add lemon juice and mix well. Place the salmon on serving dish, pour the wine mix over, and decorate with the chopped chives.

This recipe will do for smoked trout as well. It certainly does add interest to the fish if you've had a run of smoking, and are getting a little bored with the flavour.

The marinade can vary by either using wine vinegar or herb vinegar instead of wine. Tarragon vinegar is good, but use half the quantity, and baste salmon during the pickling time. Turn once to ensure it is well covered and marinated.

Smoked Trout or Salmon Flan

As with most of these recipes, the fish is interchangeable. Smoked trout of course is cheaper or you may have your own smoked fish to hand. This is a nice French recipe.

Rich shortcrust pastry
8 oz smoked trout/salmon
4 oz pink mushrooms
$\frac{1}{4}$ pint cream
1 egg, beaten
Seasoning
Pinch of mace
Butter for frying

Roll out pastry thinly and line a shallow flan case, but reserve enough for a lid. Slice the mushrooms thinly and fry lightly in the butter. Flake fish into small pieces and beat into the egg. Add the cream, mushrooms and butter they were cooked in, seasoning and mace. Mix well. It should not be too runny. Put into pastry case and cover with lid.

Bake at 375°F for 35–40 minutes.

Garnish with lemon slices and fresh parsley.

Smoked Trout Mousse

4 smoked trout fillets boned and skinned
½ pint soured cream
1 tablespoon of hot horseradish sauce
1 sachet gelatine
Juice of 2 lemons
Freshly ground black pepper

Flake the trout flesh and mix with the sour cream. Dissolve the gelatine in the lemon juice, and stand the cup in a bowl of boiling water to melt. When liquid, add to fish mixture, beat well, with the horseradish and black pepper to taste.

If bulk is needed, the well beaten white of an egg will certainly increase the volume without losing any flavour.

Pour into suitable mould. Chill in the fridge, or alternatively this will freeze well. To serve, turn out of mould, dipping into hot water if necessary.

Garnish with watercress or cucumber, and

serve with brown hot toast.

As smoked trout is salty anyway, don't add salt unless tasted beforehand, and found wanting.

A variation this recipe stands up to very well is to substitute cottage cheese for the soured cream.

Smoked Trout Paté

This is an unusual one and lovely on a hot summer's day for lunch. The raw apple makes an interesting texture.

1 large smoked trout (2 fillets)
¼ lb butter
¼ pint soured cream
1 crisp apple (we use Granny Smiths)
Juice from 2 lemons
Freshly ground black pepper

Skin and bone fish if necessary, flake with a fork. Soften butter for easy mixing. Grate the apple and cover with the lemon juice, to keep its colour. If a blender is to be used, put all the ingredients in and blend until smooth. I beat until well mixed, not too smooth for our taste. Serve with a simple crisp salad and brown bread and butter. Add more lemon if required, although the lemon in the paté should be sufficient. Watercress (if fresh) would be as good as a salad and does add eye appeal.

Terrine of Trout from the Whitwell 'Noel Arms'

This recipe is a lovely compromise between English and French cuisine. Nick's two years at a top French restaurant were well worthwhile!

Trout
White Wine
Fish stock (preferably cods heads, sole trimmings and prawn shells)
Shallots

Clean and gut trout. Poach lightly in white wine, with chopped shallots and previously prepared fish stock. When cool enough to handle bone and skin fish, and pass through mincer twice, or put in blender.

Then for a pound of fish you need

2 egg whites whipped until stiff
½ pint of double cream
Squeeze of lemon juice
Brandy to taste
Reduced fish stock
½ pint peeled prawns
Seasoning

Fold egg whites into the smooth fish, using a light action. Then just as carefully add the double cream. Add lemon juice, brandy and seasoning and enough reduced fish stock to get a dropping consistency.

Put half the mixture into a suitable dish (terrine if possible). Now add the peeled prawns, making a nice colourful layer, and cover with the rest of the trout. Seal with oiled foil. Place in a baking tray with hot water half way up the dish (bain-marie). Bake in a pre-heated oven, 350°F for ¾ hour. If a skewer comes away from the middle clean then it is cooked.

To serve it hot, serve with fingers of toast, and a lobster sauce.

To serve cold, keep cool for 2 days preferably, to allow it to set. Serve with salad and mayonnaise.

Avocado and Curried Trout

Cold trout
2 tablespoon mayonnaise
2 tablespoon sour cream
Avocado
Dash of curry powder (mild)
Lime juice

Carefully bone and flake fish. Mix mayonnaise and sour cream together with literally a dash of curry powder, enough to just colour the cream mix, and give a very subtle curry flavour. Fold in the fish.

Chill until almost ready to serve. Cut the avocado in half and brush with the lime juice, after removing the stone. Fill with curry mix.

Garnish with lime slices, and serve at once.

Trout with Orange Salad

Lemon and lime are the usual juices to go with fish dishes.

Especially in winter the Spanish Navel oranges are superb, and lovely in any salad. The iceberg lettuces and peeled and neatly sliced oranges go down well with any of the cold fish recipes.

Diced cold fresh/smoked trout or salmon served on an orange and crisp lettuce bed with slices of avocado and/or melon balls. The juice of an orange is mixed into a delicate mayonnaise and served separately.

Chives finely chopped, or the tops of spring onions minutely chopped are the only garnish needed.

Trout or Salmon Vol-au-Vents

This is a variation of a Victorian dish frequently served at their grand functions, but instead of lobster, uses neatly flaked trout or salmon 'left overs'. If you are doing a buffet for a lot of people, it is worth poaching a fish just for it, as the sauce is rather special. At the same time if is flavoursome enough to add something to an out of condition fish.

1 lb puff pastry (frozen will do if you are busy) or ready prepared vol-au-vent cases if liked
½ lb cooked and neatly flaked trout or salmon
¼ pint double cream
½ pint very thick béchamel sauce, with grated nutmeg
¼ lb pink mushrooms
1 glass of dry sherry or white wine
24 prawns cooked
Fresh parsley sprigs for garnish
Butter for cooking mushrooms
Salt and pepper

Bake pastry cases and allow to cool. (Quantities given are enough for 24 cases.)

Melt butter in pan until bubbling. Add neatly sliced mushrooms and just lightly sauté. Add mushrooms and flaked fish into the still warm béchamel sauce. Add the cream beaten with sherry (we like the Manzanilla with its slightly salty taste that seems to go so well with fish). Season to taste. Fill the vol-au-vents with this mixture. Do not be afraid to taste for seasoning, and adjust for personal taste. Pop a shelled prawn on top of each filled vol-au-vent before putting on a lid at an angle to show prawn beneath. Put into an already heated oven 300°F for 5 minutes. Decorate with a small parsley sprig on each case.

Smoked Trout Soup

This tasty soup only takes a little smoked trout (left-overs perhaps?), but it is easy to make, and satisfying to eat.

½ lb of smoked trout (approx) flaked, more if possible
1 pint of milk
1 bay leaf
¼ pint fish stock (cube if necessary)
1 oz butter
1 oz flour
Generous amount of chopped parsley
Garlic croûtons
Seasoning if required

Boil milk with bayleaf and put on one side. Melt butter in another pan and add flour, and when incorporated, pour the milk over and bring to the boil, stirring all the time. Add the flaked fish. If you like a smooth soup, purée at this stage. Add fish stock. Check for seasoning.

Make croûtons, drain on kitchen paper.

Reheat soup carefully. Sprinkle with parsley just before serving. Serve croûtons separately.

8 Regional Dishes

Salmon Cutlets Cooked in Red Wine

We always seem to think that fish should have white wine to go with it, but the French do have an alternative method that is certainly worth trying, especially if you like Burgundy.

6 salmon cutlets (or one per person)
6 evenly sized mushrooms (optional)
½ pint red Burgundy
¼ pint fish stock (stock cube if necessary)
¼ pint double cream
Salt and pepper to taste
Butter for cooking

Well butter a thick frying pan. Have the cutlets of even size. Place in the pan, and cover with the Burgundy, and very gently poach until cooked, being very careful not to break them. Place on a warmed serving dish. Add the stock to the wine the fish was cooked in, and simmer until reduced to approximately ½ a pint. Pour the cream into this liquid and bring to the simmer. Don't let it boil. Season to taste, strain and pour over the cutlets. Top each one with lightly sautéd mushroom if using them.

Serve with a nice green vegetable *al dente*, (sliced green beans or mange tout peas go well) and very creamy mashed potatoes, garnished with finely chopped parsley or chives. My husband will have finished the Burgundy off by the time the meal is ready so make sure you have two bottles.

Two Recipes From the Falcon Hotel, Uppingham

What a beautiful place and what beautiful food.

Rutland Trout with Champagne Sauce and Tropical Fruits

Lightly season trout with freshly chopped thyme, salt and pepper. Poach trout either side in a little champagne until cooked, then keeping trout warm use a reduction of the stock to make sauce. Use same method as Hollandaise Sauce. Beat egg yolks into reduction until creamy and add warm melted butter, pour sauce over fish and garnish with thin slithers of tropical fruits (kiwi, mango, pineapple, white peach). Note the different colours in fruit!

Fresh Salmon with Sage and Served en Croûte

Season salmon with a little lemon juice, freshly chopped sage also a little chopped parsley. Salt and pepper. Seal salmon into a puff pastry case and bake in moderate oven. This way all the flavour of the herbs are cooked into the salmon. For the sauce, reduce the fish stock (preferably from salmon head and bone), add Noilly Prat and then reduce with cream until good consistency. Serve salmon on top of sauce and garnish with fresh watercress and a small crayfish.

Trout Breton

This recipe is very easy to do, but does have a professional touch, as anyone who has dined at the 'Candlesticks' at Stamford will recognise

Whole trout
Fresh herbs, finely chopped
Lemon juice
Seasoned Flour
Prawns
Butter for cooking
Sliced mushrooms
Glass of white wine
Seasoning to taste
Purëed onion an optional extra

Clean and gut trout and coat with seasoned flour.

Heat butter in thick frying pan, saute mushrooms and prawns in butter, and put on one side. Put trout in pan and saute, cook over fairly low heat for 10 minutes or so, according to size. Add wine, finely chopped herbs, lemon juice, and sautéd prawns and mushrooms, and heat through.

An alternative version of this which is very convenient if you have guests, is as follows.

Sauté prawns and mushrooms. Have some buttered foil, place trout on it, and cover with mushrooms and prawns. Pour over wine, add herbs, lemon juice and seasoning. Seal foil parcel tightly and cook in a preheated oven 375°F for 30 minutes. It won't spoil if left in turned down oven until ready.

Mr. Pinto at the 'Candlesticks' recommends trying the purëed onion, especially in the foil-wrapped trout.

Haycock Baked Trout

Trout 12 oz approx
$\frac{1}{4}$ pint white wine
12 black olives
6 nice shell-on prawns
Anchovy slices optional
1 bay leaf
1 shallot
12 oz tin of tomatoes
Butter for cooking
} Tomato Concasse
Seasoning
$\frac{1}{2}$ lemon
Parsley for garnish

The Tomato Concasse can be made any time during the day. Chop the shallot and sweat in a pan with the butter, add the tinned tomatoes and reduce to a nice thick purée, check this for seasoning.

You can leave this until needed.

Richard Brandrick, the Kitchen Manager, insists an earthenware dish should be used for this recipe, to keep in line with his traditional cooking.

Grease the dish with butter, place fish in centre, cover with tomato purée, add the white wine, put olives round. Cover with tin foil. Place in preheated oven 375°F for approximately 30 minutes.

Take out and place the prawns shell on still, on top, and an anchovy fillet in between prawns if using them.

Garnish with lemon slices and parsley.

This recipe is very adaptable using either larger fish to suit your particular requirements, or try it with red mullet.

Italian Trout

4 small Trout
4 sprigs fresh lemon thyme
4 slices Parma ham
Juice of one lemon
2 oz butter
Salt and Pepper

Clean and gut trout, wash and pat dry. Place a sprig of thyme in each fish. Squeeze the lemon juice over each trout. Grease 4 sheets of foil with the butter. Wrap a slice of ham round each trout and season inside. Make foil parcel of each fish, making sure each parcel is leak proof. Put the parcels on a baking tray. Bake in pre-heated oven, temperature 400°F for the first 10 minutes. Lower heat to 350° and bake for a further 10 minutes, or a bit longer if the fish are on the plump side.

Serve a parcel unopened to each guest, as the aroma is the important thing in opening these foil wrapped fish. Brown bread and butter is often quite enough to have with these trout.

Portuguese Baked Trout

('Bull & Swan', Stamford, Lincs.)

This area is so spoilt: it has an abundance of good eating places, and the difficulty is deciding which one. However, a lot of people when in doubt go to the Bull and Swan, with its quality, quantity and service. Here is one of their ways of cooking trout.

1 trout per person
1 onion, diced
2 tomatoes, chopped
½ green pepper, diced
1 glass white wine
1 clove of garlic, crushed
Salt and pepper to taste
Tin foil

Clean and gut trout, lay it on the top of the foil, put all ingredients on the trout (don't lose the wine), and seal into the foil. Place parcel on baking tray.

Cook in hot oven, 375°F for 20 minutes.

Spanish Trout

Spain, like France, has excellent game fishing, and the areas are beautiful and bear little likeness to the sun seekers idea of Spain. Here is a simple little recipe from Spain which has the aroma of mediterranean cooking.

4 small trout
2 cloves of garlic (the Spanish use 6)
5 tablespoons wine vinegar
2 sprigs of parsley
1 teaspoon salt
1 teaspoon paprika
Good pinch of white pepper

Gut trout and fillet, cutting off the fins. Then wash in clean water, pat dry with kitchen towelling. Cut each fillet in half. Peel and chop garlic. Place trout fillets in a saucepan, add garlic, oil, vinegar, paprika, salt and pepper. Place over high heat, and when boiling point is reached turn heat down to simmering level for 10 minutes.

Trout cooked like this makes an excellent starter. Serve it hot or cold.

I have reduced the garlic, but if you are up to 6 cloves, then I think it better to use them.

A lovely Rioja dry wine does go well with this, but so does a good sherry like the Manzanilla, which is a good one and will take you right through the meal.

Chinese Steamed Trout

As Chinese food is very much 'in' at the moment, this recipe is interesting.

Trout, small 1 per person
½ lb button mushrooms
4 spring onions
4 tablespoons groundnut oil
Soy sauce. 2 tablespoons
Dash of dry white wine (Chinese if possible)
Cornflour small teaspoonful
Seasoning
Small piece of ginger peeled and grated

Clean and gut trout, wipe dry. Slice mushrooms, flatten and then slice onions. Place fish on a suitable dish and place on a stand in wok, or on a rack in a large saucepan. Cover with the vegetables and sprinkle the ginger all over.

Mix the groundnut oil, soy sauce, cornflour, wine and seasoning together and pour over fish.

Steam over rapidly boiling water covered with a tightly fitting lid for about 15 minutes.

Meanwhile cook rice of your choice and snow peas (mange-tout) quickly stir fried.

Remove dish from steamer or wok and serve with rice and vegetables at once.

Suffolk Trout

Suffolk is not very well endowed with rivers or streams, but the traditional way they cooked trout was almost as they cooked herring when I was very young.

4 trout
2 oz butter
4 bay leaves
juice of a lemon
Seasoning

Clean and gut the trout and take heads off. Pop a bay leaf inside each fish with a twist of pepper and salt. Melt butter in a thick frying pan. Put the trout in when the butter is bubbling. Add the lemon juice over fish. Cover, turn heat down and cook slowly, turning once. Serve very hot with petit pois and either small potatoes or potato balls tossed in a little butter.

Garnish with parsley.

Hot Mousseline of Rutland Water Pike with Crabmeat

Ingredients to make about 1 lb or 6 little darioles

½ lb pike fillets skinned and boned
Salt
Cayenne pepper
Paprika
3 large egg whites
¾ pint of double cream
Meat from 2 small fresh crabs or 1 large crab
1 carrot
1 onion
6 shallots
1 bunch fresh tarragon
1 bay leaf
2 celery stalks
1 leek
3 tomatoes
1 glass of white wine
2 oz unsalted butter
Sherry vinegar (two tablespoons full)

In a mortar or food processor work the fish with the egg whites to a smooth purée, season with salt and cayenne pepper. Pass the fish through a fine sieve into a mixing bowl to remove any bones and fibres. Place the mixing bowl with the sieved fish in it on a bed of crushed ice in a larger mixing bowl.

With a wooden spoon beat the mixture vigorously, gradually incoporating half a pint of cream. Continue beating the mixture for a few more minutes.

Make a little 'quenelle' the size of a pigeon's egg with a teaspoon and poach it for 5 minutes to test for seasoning and consistency. It should be light and fluffy and hold its shape. If too light it will crumble and can only be cured by stirring your mousseline into one with slightly more fish content. If too heavy it can be lightened by the addition of cream. Place the mousseline into the refrigerator.

Plunge the live crabs into boiling salted water and boil vigorously for 20 minutes (large) or 10–15 minutes (small). Keep the water in which the crabs have been boiled for future use in the sauce.

Remove the meat from the crab claws and set aside. Open the crab, remove the 'dead mens fingers' from around the inside of the body of the crab and discard.

To make the crab sauce, chop the carcase and shell of the crab as finely as possible. Roast in the oven for 15 minutes sprinkled generously with paprika, finely chopped carrots, onions, shallots, tarragon, bay leaf, celery stalks, leeks, tomato and cayenne pepper. Add a glass of white wine and enough of the cooking liquor from the crabs to barely cover. Bring back to the boil and with a wooden spoon stir up as much as possible of the residue which has stuck to the bottom of the pan.

Transfer to a clean saucepan and gently simmer with the lid on for 2 hours. Strain through a coarse sieve squeezing the solids with the back of a ladle to extract as much as possible of the juices. Transfer back into the saucepan and reduce to by two thirds. Add the remaining $\frac{1}{4}$ pint cream and bring back to the boil. Reduce as much as necessary to obtain a smooth consistency thick enough to coat the back of a spoon evenly. Finish by whisking in a knob of cold unsalted butter. Adjust the seasoning and sharpness with lemon juice. Finally pass through a fine sieve and keep warm.

To cook the mousselines butter the dariole

moulds generously and spoon the mousseline mixture around the bottom and sides. Fill the centre with crabmeat and cover the hole with more mousseline. Smooth off the base of the moulds with a palette knife and cover each mould with buttered silver foil. Stand the moulds in a bain marie ¾ immersed in water and poach in a slow oven, 350°F, gas mark 4, for approximately 20 minutes or until the mixture starts to rise.

Onto the hot serving plates turn out mousselines and coat generously with the rich crab sauce. Serve immediately.

This very exciting recipe comes from Hambleton Hall. The terraced garden falls away to Rutland water. Smoked salmon never tasted better.

9 Dishes for Left-Overs

Salmon and Asparagus Flan

Do use fresh asparagus for this dish. The colour and taste are so very good and complement the delicate colouring of the salmon.

Good shortcrust pastry shell
½ lb cooked salmon
2 eggs
½ lb asparagus, cooked lightly, 3 minutes at most
½ pint single cream
Finely cut bulbs of spring onions
Pinch of mace
Seasoning

Make good shortcrust pastry and bake blind in an 8 inch flan case. Beat eggs and cream together. Bone and skin the salmon, flake, and add to the eggs and cream. Season and add mace. Keep four spears of the cooked asparagus and cut the rest into ½ inch pieces. Add these to the mixture with the finely chopped onion bulbs, and pour into the flan case, putting the whole spears decoratively on last.

Bake in a hot oven 375°F for 35–40 minutes.

Smoked salmon pieces can be used instead of fresh salmon and is equally good.

Just freshly boiled potatoes garnished with finely snipped chives is all you need to accompany this dish, but a crisp green salad is never amiss.

Trout or Salmon Soup

At one time the thought of having any salmon or trout leftover did not seem possible, but living with an angler it does happen from time to time. There is a lot to be done with these oddments. Some recipes are in the luxury class, some just fill a gap, but all taste good. The soup is very good.

If you poached the fish then you will have the stock it was cooked in.

1 pint of fish stock or more if you have it (you can always freeze surplus soup) Check for seasoning
1 stalk celery chopped
1 leek very finely sliced
¼ lb small mushrooms thinly sliced (pale ones)
¼ pint of shelled shrimps or halved prawns
5 oz dry white wine or sherry
2 oz butter
2 heaped tablespoons of flour
Cupful of leftover trout or salmon
Fresh parsley, thyme or tarragon
Seasoning to taste if necessary

If no fish stock available, don't forget the very good stock cubes available (fish of course).

Put stock into saucepan. Melt butter in frying pan (don't let it colour only bubble). Add vegetables and cook for 3–4 minutes. Strain vegetables, leaving as much of the butter in the frying pan as possible. Add vegetables to the stock, bring to the boil and simmer for 10 minutes. Now add fish and prawns or shrimps and bring back to the simmer. Stir the flour into the butter in the frying pan, mix well over low heat. When blended add the wine and stir carefully. Tip this very carefully into the soup and when blended perfectly simmer for no more than 4 minutes.

Decorate with fresh herbs. Serve with croûtons.

I think it is preferable to have the pale mushrooms for eye appeal, the dark looking ones just don't seem to go with the delicate colour of the soup.

Trout/Salmon Pancakes

Allow 2 thin pancakes per person. No sugar, only grated lemon rind.

Cold poached trout or salmon
¾ pint béchamel sauce with 2 tablespoons of tomato sauce
¼ pint of double cream
2 oz butter
Grated Parmesan cheese (optional)
Salt and pepper to taste

Makes pancakes in normal way. I like the taste of the lemon best, but it is a matter of taste. Do make them thin, like crêpes. Keep them warm.

Meanwhile heat butter in frying pan until bubbling, not brown. Turn the flaked trout in the pan until heated through. If you don't want to use the cheese you can at this point add a spoonful of herbs (tarragon, chives, or parsley).

Halve the béchamel sauce and put one half in the pan with the fish. Stir well, being careful not to break the fish up too much. Divide this mixture equally between the number of pancakes made. Put the pancakes on hot dish and keep hot while the covering sauce is made.

Add the cream to the remaining béchamel

sauce. Add the seasoning and tomato sauce and bring almost to the boil. Pour over pancakes and serve immediately, unless using the parmesan cheese, in which case sprinkle cheese evenly over the pancakes and flash under a hot grill for just long enough for the cheese to colour slightly.

Serve at once, garnished with finely chopped fresh parsley.

Spiced Trout

This is a good way to use up cold trout or salmon, and is very easy to do.

Cold trout, preferably fillets
½ pint of wine vinegar
1 teaspoon of cloves
½ teaspoon of allspice
8 peppercorns
Sea salt to taste

Mix all the ingredients (except fish) in a saucepan and boil for 2 minutes. Leave to cool. Strain and pour over fish. Put in a cool place for at least 2 hours. Drain.

Serve with a crisp salad.

Potted Trout (1)

Suitable for trout or salmon, it is delicious and will freeze well.

½ lb cold trout or salmon
¼ lb butter
Good pinch of salt, pepper and mace
Anchovy essence to taste (I use about a dessertspoon)

Flake cooked fish, remove bone and skin. Either beat or put all ingredients into blender for 2–3 minutes, or until smooth. In cold weather just soften butter first for easy mixing.

Put into attractive dish if serving straight away, or suitable container for freezing. Cover with melted butter. Chill or freeze. Cover with foil if freezing. Serve with brown bread, toast, or hot rolls.

Potted Trout (2)

½ lb cold cooked trout or salmon
¼ lb butter
3 tablespoons of horseradish sauce
Salt and pepper to taste

Beat or blend all ingredients until smooth. Put into a dish and pour over melted butter. Chill or freeze. Serve with hot toast, and lemon if wished.

If more fish available than amounts stated, just adjust other ingredients, and mix as stated.

Trout Fritters

This is a way of using up cold trout, but it does of course appeal to the younger members of the family, more than some of the recipes do.

½ lb trout (approximately) boned, skinned and flaked
2 rounded tablespoons of flour
2 eggs
¼ pint cream or, if calorie watching, top of the milk
Pinch of cayenne pepper
Sunflower or corn oil for frying

Sauce ingredients
- 4 oz butter (melted)
- Scant dessertspoon of flour
- 1 dessertspoon of soy sauce
- 1 tablespoon of tomato ketchup or anchovy essence for adult taste

Add the flour and seasoning to the flaked fish. Beat the eggs well and add these with the cream or milk to the fish mixture.

Heat the oil in a frying pan until smoking. Drop the fish batter into the pan by tablespoonfuls and fry until golden brown both sides. Drain on kitchen paper, and keep warm whilst the sauce is being cooked.

Mix the flour into the melted butter, then put over heat stirring all the time until thickened but don't let it change colour. Add the soy sauce and whichever of the flavourings being used.

As usual, chopped parsley doesn't come amiss for serving, but in our family the young ones are not too bothered if fried mushrooms are a substitute.

This is a very nice breakfast dish.

Fisherman's Omelettes

Omelettes are a delight to eat and the variety of fillings endless. They can be prepared so quickly and easily. Here are a few 'fishy' ideas.

Prepare the fillings and keep them hot while making the omelettes, so they can be served immediately. Make omelette in the usual way, using fresh herbs preferably, so you do not have to use any in the filling.

Here are a few fillings to give you some ideas:

1. Herring roes
   Very thin slices of smoked salmon
   Seasoning
   Pinch of cayenne pepper
   Butter for cooking

Season the roes and wrap a slice of salmon round each one. Gently cook in butter. Place a roll in each omelette. Serve at once.

2. Cooked trout, boned and flaked
   Few prawns or shrimps (shelled)
   Seasoning
   A little double cream
   Small scraps of nutmeg

Heat all these together gently, and fill each omelette as it is cooked.

3. Smoked trout flaked and boned
   Béchamel sauce

Mix together and heat through.

4. Avocado
   Trout or salmon, cooked and flaked
   Squeeze of lemon
   Butter for cooking
   Seasoning

Using a sharp teaspoon, cut balls of ripe avocado. Squeeze lemon over at once. Heat a little butter in a pan, add the fish and avocado balls, gently heat through.

Trout Box

Another good way of using up cooked trout.

Cold trout
1 lb long grain rice, cooked and fluffy
Salt and pepper and grated nutmeg

Line a square tin with cooked rice, fill up with the flaked fish, season well. Then cover with the rest of rice. Put foil over the dish and bake in medium oven 350°F for an hour. Turn out and serve with a good sauce, we like prawn or egg, but a favourite creamy sauce of your choice will make a filling tasty meal with little effort.

Slimmer's Pâté

½ lb cooked trout (approximately)
Carton of sour cream
Squeeze of lemon juice
Seasoning
Sherry to taste or smokey whisky
Olive or grape seed oil

Remove any skin and bone from fish and beat until smooth. Add the lemon juice, the carton of sour cream and a dribble of oil, beating all the time until the right texture. Pour in a dash of whichever alcohol you fancy. Taste for seasoning. Chill for at least 2 hours.

In these days of healthy eating, those of us who have game fish at our disposal are very lucky. We are always being told red meat can be a contributory cause of arthritis and could be a possible carcinogen. So the more interesting we make our fish dishes, and the more fish we eat, the better.

Curried Trout

This is one of the few times a strong flavour is added to a trout dish, but only enough to make it subtle. It is worthwhile when cooking trout to do an extra one just for this recipe.

Cold trout, as much as possible
1 oz butter
1 oz flour
Milk, about ½ pint
1 shallot finely chopped
Curry powder (not a hot one)
Seasoning

Flake and very carefully remove all bones. I don't skin mine.

Melt the butter in a thick pan, throw in the chopped shallot, and stir in the flour, and a heaped teaspoon of a curry powder, gradually add the milk stirring constantly. Cook 2–3 minutes then add flaked fish, turn heat down and heat through stirring gently.

Taste for curry, add a dash more if necessary, and adjust seasoning.

The flavour should be enticing not overpowering. Meanwhile cook your favourite rice. If you have a ring mould put rice into that, and invert on serving dish. Pour the curried fish sauce into centre and serve at once.

The simple basic sauce given for this dish is one that I use instead of some of the richer traditional sauces, which have too much cholesterol for today's diet.

Potted Char

These fish are highly esteemed on the continent, and served at all the top banquets. However, in England they are only found in very deep waters, in the North and rarely appear on any menu.

Cooked char (cold, but no juices)
and an equal weight of butter
Seasoning
Ground mace or nutmeg

The French cook their char and grayling on a bed of chopped shallots with a dash of wine. If cooked this way, char will have a good flavour, but do not use the juices fish are cooked in, as it will spoil the fish.

Flake the flesh finely with a fork, weigh, and add the same amount of softened butter. Add a pinch of mace, taste for seasoning, and beat all together until smooth.

Traditionally, decorative pots were used for this delicacy, but use whatever available.

Melt some more butter in a pan and pour over the potted fish, to seal completely.

Any potted fish does need a protective covering of foil to prevent the butter seal shrinking away from the edges, if being frozen.

Serve with thin brown bread and butter, with a crisp white wine to drink.

Salmon Roe

If the fish is to be smoked, some smokehouses will smoke the roe if asked, but if self catering the roe can be gently poached, in salted water, with lemon juice and peel, for 15–20 minutes. Lift out when cool enough to handle, and press between two plates, the top one weighted, and leave for several hours.

It can be eaten cold, or better still cut into 1″ slices and then fried with bacon for breakfast.

Appendix

Conversion Tables

ENGLISH MEASURES

1 pint	= 20 fluid oz	= 568 cc
1 gill	= 5 fluid oz ($\frac{1}{4}$ pint)	= 142 cc
Bottle Table wine	= 24 fluid oz	= 680 cc
1 pound (lb)	= 16 oz	

AMERICAN MEASURES

1 pint	= 16 fluid oz	= 453 cc
1 cup	= 8 fluid oz	= 227 cc
$\frac{1}{2}$ cup	= 4 tablespoons of fluid	
1 cup butter	= 5 oz	= 142 gms
1 cup grated cheese	= $3\frac{1}{2}$ oz	= 98 gms
1 cup sugar	= $7\frac{1}{2}$ oz	= 223 gms
1 cup flour	= $4\frac{1}{2}$ oz	= 128 gms

FLUIDS

1 litre = 35 fluid oz = $1\frac{3}{4}$ pints (almost exactly)
$\frac{1}{2}$ litre = $17\frac{1}{2}$ fluid oz
1 litre = 1000 cc (or ml – millimetres)

METRIC WEIGHTS

1 kilogramme	= 2·2046 lb = 2 lb $3\frac{1}{4}$ oz
7 grammes	= $\frac{1}{4}$ oz
14 grammes	= $\frac{1}{2}$ oz
21 grammes	= $\frac{3}{4}$ oz
28 grammes	= 1 oz
$453\frac{1}{2}$ grammes	= 1 lb

OVEN TEMPERATURES

	Degrees Fahrenheit	*Regulo*	*Degrees Centigrade*
Very slow	200 – 280	$\frac{1}{4}$ – $\frac{1}{2}$	115 – 135
Slow	280 – 320	1	135 – 160
Warm	320 – 340	3	160 – 170
Moderate	340 – 370	4	170 – 185
Fairly hot	370 – 400	5 – 6	185 – 205
Hot	400 – 440	7	205 – 225
Very hot	440 – 500	8 – 9	225 – 250

Index